A Year for Wisdom

For a new year full of challenges we cannot yet see, let us ask God for the gift of wise and discerning hearts, so that we can live well and discern between right and wrong.

We begin the year with readings in Proverbs, a book of wisdom. Solomon, as a new king, begged the Lord for wisdom over and above any gift of wealth or power (1 Kings 3). Living in 2024, we can do no better than follow his example in asking for God's help to discern our times and seeking that same divine spiritual gift. To have wisdom is to have the mind of Christ as we make choices; and to see with his eyes and hear with his ears as we encounter others.

I am so grateful each quarter to our writers, who pray, study and prepare our notes with such diligence and faith. Each brings his or her wisdom and experience to the reading of the Word of God. In this quarter, I am reminded that it is easy to substitute other, easier, things for the 'one thing necessary' – the pursuit of God. Whether we explore the stories of the kings of Israel and Judah, the mission of the church in Acts, the way of faithfulness described in Ephesians or the challenges facing the disciples in the final days of Jesus' earthly life, we are faced with the same choice. Will I, today, be wise with my time, my devotion and my life? Lord, give me wisdom to serve and follow you.

We also come to the end of our *Bible Unpacked* series with David Smith's overview of apocalyptic writing. This series was intended to help us to see the different kinds of literature that make up our Bible. Our contributors, drawn from different specialisations, have given us a feast for which we are grateful. In the next issue we will begin a new series – watch this space!

Every blessing as you embark on the adventure of 2024. May the reading of God's Word be your wisdom and strength.

Sally Nelson
Editor

Angela Grigson
Senior Content Manager

ON THE COVER: '... hope is renewed that the ultimate triumph belongs to Israel's God and his Messiah' (pages 66 to 69)

Image credit: iStock / borchee

The Writers

ROBERT PARKINSON is minister of Didsbury Baptist Church, Manchester and an associate tutor for Northern Baptist College. He is a keen student of the Bible with special interest in the Old Testament.

DANIEL MCGINNIS is the Principal of St Hild College and leads the Sheffield Centre. He is also the Founder of the Leeds School of Theology. He loves the book of Acts, and has a passion for seeing today's church inspired by the earliest church. He also enjoys teaching theology, particularly New Testament studies and hermeneutics.

ALISON LO is retiring in her home city, Hong Kong after being abroad for more than two decades. She has been an Old Testament faculty lecturer at the Chinese University of Hong Kong, London School of Theology, Singapore Baptist Theological Seminary and Bethel Seminary (MN).

DAVID HORSFALL is the Director of Leeds School of Theology. He is also an associate lecturer at St Hild College and CYM. He is currently studying for a PhD in theology at Durham University with a focus on New Testament studies.

BRIAN RADCLIFFE is a retired English and Drama teacher, formerly minister of a Baptist church in the north of England. Also enjoys a parallel career as freelance writer (secondary assembly scripts/drama skills as cross-curricula teaching tools).

DAVID SMITH is an honorary lecturer at the University of Aberdeen, and is active in teaching and writing. He is currently researching a book entitled *God or Mammon: Choice of the Century*.

SALLY NELSON is the Dean of Baptist Formation at St Hild College, Yorkshire, UK, where she also teaches Christian doctrine and pastoral care. She is a Baptist minister and has been the commissioning editor for *Encounter with God* since 2015.

Contents

Scripture Union is a member of the worldwide Scripture Union international community.
Website: https://scriptureunion.global

CHANGED BY FAITH

Through your support, SU trained church pastors Lox and Ruth Busisa as Faith Guides so they could support young people without church backgrounds to explore the Bible and encounter and respond to Jesus. Being part of their group changed the life of teenager Ali in ways she never would have dreamed.

Lox and Ruth lead LifePoint Church Pembrokeshire, located on a deprived estate in Haverfordwest. During the pandemic, SU helped them to connect with young people in the community through setting up regular sports ministry in the local park. On Sundays, they would have a short vibrant service, Church in the Park, open to all. 'That's when we first met Sammi and two of her children, Ali and Ethan,' says Lox. 'We got to know

them and that autumn when we started a Friday group to connect with local teenagers Ali was among the ten young people who joined.'

A life-changing adventure in Kenya
Ali, then a shy girl in her early teens, had been going to a church youth group previously, but it had disbanded. At Church in the Park, she heard how Lox and Ruth had founded their own charity in Kenya where Lox was from, and how they planned to take a group of teens from Haverfordwest to help work on projects there. 'Someone said that I should come too,' recalls Ali. 'But I'd never even left Pembrokeshire, I was terrified of flying and I had no idea how I would raise the £1,500 needed!'

Raising funds at a time when COVID restrictions really limited opportunities was indeed a challenge, but Ali rose to the occasion. 'I managed to get to £1,000,' she says, 'but two weeks before the deadline, I was still £500 short of my target. I prayed and the whole church prayed with and for me.

'A few days later someone made an anonymous donation to my bank of £500. I could go to Kenya and I was just so excited!

'Out in Kenya, our team helped build part of a disabled toilet and put filters into a water tank to give the village clean water. We distributed sports equipment to local people, and just helped out in the community however we could. It was amazing to see what Ruth and Lox do there, and to see God's help in that. And the worship at the churches was amazing!

'I knew about Christianity before, but it was only after going to Kenya and seeing and experiencing faith in action that I wanted to make a commitment and be baptised.'

Many more prayers answered!
Ali continued to experience God's presence on her return as she sat school exams. 'I get really stressed in exams but the church said they'd pray for me. In the exams I would pray for God's help, and the answers would just come to me. I passed all my exams, which I really didn't expect!'

Ali also used to get bullied at school, which had robbed her of her self-confidence. Ali, together with Lox, Ruth and the rest of the church, prayed that she would get a Christian friend. 'Soon after,' says Ali, 'a girl called Tanatswa joined our year group in school. She was from Zimbabwe, and our teacher asked me to introduce her to other people and look after her. The first thing Tanatswa asked me was, "Are there any churches in Haverfordwest?" She was a Christian! So I brought her along to church, and she's been a really good friend to me.'

Tanatswa's welcome friendship was one of the many answers to prayer that God has given Ali.

Fearfully and wonderfully made

Tanatswa and Ali both go to Lox and Ruth's Rooted youth group on a Wednesday evening. SU would term it as a Grow Community, meaning that most of the young people believe in Jesus but don't come from a church background as such. Ruth leads the group and says, 'The group are really open to exploring faith and ask lots of great questions. We have worship, Bible study and prayer, which our young people love – they are amazed they can speak to God and he hears! We use the SU Rooted journals to spark discussion and discover more about God and faith.'

Recently, Lox spoke to the group on Psalm 139. He says, 'I explained how the Bible says we are "fearfully and wonderfully made". At school, it's all about popularity – how many views you get on TikTok, how many likes you get on Instagram. But it's dependent on getting your clothes, make-up, hair, and so on right, in line with the latest trends which can change overnight. That constant need to compete and live up to some sort of unrealistic expectation messes them up.

'He doesn't look at their make-up, their hair, how they dress, their social media ratings. He sees through all those layers and loves them anyway, with a love that doesn't change.'

'But I told them how God thinks they're awesome as they are. He doesn't look at their make-up, their hair, how they dress, their social media ratings. He sees through all those layers and loves them anyway, with a love that doesn't change.

'You could sense their relief. To know that God loves them, whatever their popularity rating, is something very unique and precious for them to be aware of and to hold on to, especially in these times of so much change.'

'Knowing God has changed me'

Ali agrees wholeheartedly. 'I used to wear lots of make-up and try and be who other people wanted me to be, rather than being myself.

'But knowing God has changed me. I'm learning to accept and to value the person he made me to be. My mum says I've blossomed. I've certainly grown in confidence. Even last year I would never have thought I could stand at the front of church and give a talk to lots of people – but now I can and I have! And I've helped run church events for over 60 children.'

When she turns 17, Ali hopes to go as a young leader on SLAM, a short sports-based residential on the Gower which is organised by SU Mission Enabler Jack Newbould. Faith Guides bring groups of young people on it, and Ali was one of the teenagers that Lox and Ruth brought when it started in 2021.

Ali knows that God has a plan for her future, and it's a future that she's excited about! 'I used to dream of going to America and having my own YouTube channel and a big following, but God has given me a real change of heart. Now more than anything I want to study health, social care and sociology, and become a mental health nurse.'

Please pray that God continues to guide and bless Ali, that she will grow in faith and knowledge of him, and in turn help inspire other young people to discover the God who loves them and accepts them – just as they are.

A shorter version of this story first appeared in *Connecting You*, SU's free quarterly supporter magazine. If you'd like to receive copies of *Connecting You* and learn more of how God is moving in the hearts and lives of children and young people today, you can sign up online at su.org.uk/connectingyou.

Using this Guide

Encounter with God is designed for thinking Christians who want to interpret and apply the Bible in a way that is relevant to the problems and issues of today's world. It is based on the NIV translation of the Bible, but can easily be used with any other version.

Each set of readings begins with an *Introduction* to the section you are about to study. The *Call to Worship* section at the start of each note should help you consciously to come into God's presence before you read the passage. The main *Explore* section aims to bring out the riches hidden in the text. The *Growing in Faith* section at the end suggests ways of applying the message to daily living.

The *Bible in a Year* readings at the foot of the page are for those who want this additional option.

IN SEARCH OF WISDOM

The book of Proverbs is often thought of as a compendium of short, sharp and largely unconnected sayings conveying traditional wisdom and common sense. However, chapters 1–9 and 31 are different, containing lengthier, sustained arguments on wisdom-related themes. The first nine chapters function as an introduction to the book, helping to orient the reader to the material that follows.

Chapter 1 begins, 'The proverbs of Solomon son of David, king of Israel'. This may refer to the whole book or just to chapters 1–9. Either way, the proverbs are associated in some way with Solomon. This may mean he wrote them, but it is just as likely that they were collected through many years of Israelite history, then presented in honour of King Solomon, whose name had already become associated with the genre.

Much of Proverbs 1–9 takes the form of an address written from a parent to a young man setting out in life with a lot to learn. The address, 'my son', occurs 15 times. On such occasions, those of us who are not young Israelite males are invited to use our imagination, to put ourselves in the sandals of the addressee and extrapolate warning and advice for our own circumstances. These chapters are bookended with 'The fear of the LORD is the beginning of knowledge/wisdom' (see 1:7; 9:10) and they contain some of the most loved sayings of the Bible. Wisdom is sometimes personified, most obviously in chapter 8, where Wisdom is presented as a woman of high standing. I try to use the capitalised 'Wisdom' whenever I think the personal form is in view. I hope that, as we read these chapters, we shall rediscover a vital resource for our own growth in wisdom and understanding.

Robert Parkinson

FOR FURTHER READING

Ellen F Davis, *Proverbs, Ecclesiastes, and the Song of Songs*, Westminster John Knox Press, 2000
Michael V Fox, *Proverbs 1–9*, Yale University Press, 2000
Ernest C Lucas, *Proverbs*, Eerdmans, 2015

The Fear of the Lord

Lord, help me in the coming year to lean not on my own understanding but in all my ways to submit to you, that you might make my ways straight.[1]

The idea of fearing God is distinctly out of fashion for many today, but I want to say something in favour of it! Proverbs, after all, is unequivocal. 'The fear of the LORD is the beginning of knowledge' (v 7).[2] Now, let me acknowledge that there is a kind of fear of God that has nothing to do with a God of love and that no Christian would want to own. I mean the cringing fear that would turn us away from God in terror and dread. This is not the fear recommended by the book of Proverbs. On the contrary, the kind of fear Proverbs has in mind would draw us towards God in reverent appreciation and awe-filled gratitude.

At its most basic, the fear of God may involve the recognition that we live our lives before a living God who will call us to account. This provides a dampener for certain courses of action and an incentive for others. Still, perhaps we need a better English word for fear when we use it in relation to God. 'Reverence', 'awe', 'respect', 'wonder' or 'amazement' are suitable candidates.

Whatever word we choose, we should recognise that God is Creator and we are his creatures. Such a recognition is basic to wise living. For when we are aware of our own creatureliness, we begin to see ourselves as fellow creatures with all of God's creation. We begin to realise that we are dependent on God and on God's world for our very existence. We begin to live more respectfully not only towards God but also towards all other creatures, both human and non-human. Such a mindset should keep us from the foolish, violent acts by which the wicked make a trap for themselves (vs 7b,10–19).

Go for a New Year's Day walk and reflect on whether you see yourself as a fellow creature to all the other creatures of God's world.

[1] See Prov 3:5,6   [2] Cf Prov 9:10

BIBLE IN A YEAR: **Genesis 1,2; Acts 1**

To Listen is to Live

'Speak, Lord, in the stillness / while I wait on thee; / hushed my heart to listen / in expectancy.'[1]

Years ago, the BBC published a magazine called *The Listener*. In the days when the BBC was entirely a radio broadcaster it referred at its most basic level to the listeners of radio. However, it also promoted a kind of approach, a posture, of listening and it appealed to an audience who thought of themselves as open to learning new things. Well, you may remember the publication and you may or may not have liked it, but that is beside the point. I am interested in the idea of a truly listening audience and in the posture of listening as one to which we might aspire.

Listening seems to be at the very heart of the wisdom that Proverbs is seeking to inculcate. 'Out in the open wisdom calls aloud, she raises her voice in the public square; at noisy street corners she cries out' (vs 20,21, footnote). Here, Wisdom is personified as a woman of high standing. The question is, will anyone listen? Will anyone notice her voice, give her the time of day and pay attention to her?

We might reply that this is all too easy for the imagined audience of a personified Wisdom, but wisdom does not really cry out in the street. Her doing so here is just a literary device to help us think about the wise and the foolish. Yet, I think a little more is intended. The passage suggests that true wisdom is not esoteric. It is not reserved for a special group with a secret code or special knowledge. It can be found in ordinary, everyday, public places and is available to all, at the price of opening our ears and paying attention: 'whoever listens to me', says Wisdom, 'will live' (v 33).

Is there someone you are not really listening to? Take some time to listen deeply to them; it might advance your relationship and spread a little wisdom in the process.

---

[1] Emily May Crawford, 1864–1927, 'Speak, Lord, in the stillness'

BIBLE IN A YEAR: **Genesis 3,4; Acts 2**

Proverbs 2

Hidden Treasure

'Your face, LORD, I will seek. Do not hide your face from me'.[1]

Wisdom, says Proverbs, is like silver, or hidden treasure (v 4). For me, this has at least two connotations. First, wisdom is extremely valuable. Essential for making beneficial choices or knowing what to do in perplexing situations, it is a treasure of inestimable worth. Second, hidden treasure does not give up its rewards unless we search for it diligently. We all know that mining can be an extremely perilous and difficult enterprise in our own day. It was even more so in ancient times. Just imagine trying to dig without any of the tools and technologies of the modern world! Wisdom, then, like silver or hidden treasure, is of great value and is worthy of our very best efforts to attain it.

Perhaps this would be true for any kind of wisdom. However, the wisdom of the book of Proverbs is a certain kind of wisdom. Though it may encompass common sense, scientific knowledge and emotional intelligence, it also has a moral quality. It involves 'what is right and just and fair' (v 9). This wisdom comes from God (v 6), from seeking God and following in God's ways. Thus, the greatest scientist in the world, were he or she to lack kindness or compassion, though possessing all the knowledge it were possible to know, still would not possess the wisdom of Proverbs. For the wisdom taught by Proverbs issues in a 'good life', made known by 'deeds done in … humility'.[2] According to James, this 'wisdom that comes from heaven is first of all pure; then peace-loving, considerate, submissive, full of mercy and good fruit, impartial and sincere'.[3] This may look to all the world like foolishness, but it is 'wiser than human wisdom'[4] and is worth seeking with every fibre of our being.

Take a few minutes to reflect on your most treasured possessions. What are they? Do they have any connection to the wisdom that comes from God?

---

[1] Ps 27:8,9 [2] James 3:13 [3] James 3:17 [4] 1 Cor 1:25

BIBLE IN A YEAR: **Genesis 5,6; Acts 3**

The Paths of Peace

Lord, help me to leave behind my foolish ways and walk in the way of insight.[1]

The governing image of the book of Proverbs is that of walking or travelling along a path, a way or a road. Life is like a journey, says Proverbs, and the character, quality and destination of your life is determined by the decisions and behaviours you adopt. Such decisions and behaviours are seen as paths, ways or roads. Wisdom is a way, a direction of life, a following along the right path, a journeying, a walking with God.

Still, this leaves me with a question. Does Proverbs 1–9 hold out any hope for people like me when I have missed the wise path and acted foolishly? I am thinking of one specific occasion when I grievously offended a friend. When I became aware of my error, I hated myself for it. I felt like a fool. For months I lost self-confidence. I just wanted to crawl into a hole and give up. I believed in the forgiveness of God, but I could not forgive myself and the book of Proverbs did not greatly help. It seemed to confirm that I was indeed an unwise fool!

Then I came anew to verses 5 and 6 of this chapter: 'Trust in the LORD with all your heart and lean not on your own understanding; in all your ways submit to him, and he will make your paths straight.' God could straighten out my paths and put me back on his way. Slowly but surely, I found the strength to go on. I had gained a little humility. No longer wise in my own eyes, I began to trust the Lord again. I discovered that there is a wisdom in being kind to oneself, in making room for one's own failings. For, wisdom's 'ways are pleasant ways, and all her paths are peace' (v 17).

Do you need to forgive yourself? Could you talk to someone about it? Whatever you do, be kind to yourself as you journey towards well-being.

[1] See Prov 9:6

BIBLE IN A YEAR: **Genesis 7,8; Psalms 1,2**

Proverbs 3:19–35

Creative Acts of Kindness

O God, fill me today with your wisdom, that I might please you in all that I do.[1]

Did you know that the early church found the Christmas story foreshadowed in the book of Proverbs? Today's passage, for example, speaks of wisdom as the creative energy that once formed the universe and is now available to human beings. This wisdom that comes down from God is much like the journey of the eternal Word made flesh. Perhaps Luke had Proverbs 3 in mind when he declared that the child Jesus 'was filled with wisdom, and the grace of God was on him'[2] and, again, 'Jesus increased in wisdom and in years, and in divine and human favour'.[3]

Now, there is a kind of wily wisdom in our world that we would not want to associate with Jesus. This is the clever wisdom that seeks to get one over on other people. This is not the sort of wisdom we find in Proverbs. There, wisdom has an ethical, neighbour-regarding quality.

This is because a world-creating energy must inspire actions that are constructive or upbuilding, not hateful, violent or destructive. Yet, Proverbs does not seek from its readers super-saintly behaviour. It does not call us to what is impossible. It does not even call us to what is heroic. It simply calls for basic human decency. 'Do not accuse anyone for no reason – when they have done you no harm' (v 30). What could be easier than that?

The wisdom that Proverbs seeks to inculcate, though high, rich and glorious, is not beyond anybody. It is attainable. It is reachable, doable, to any who will give a little time to its cultivation. It is available to the immature and the inexperienced and can be built up daily by anyone who will listen, really pay attention, to the Proverbs and let their actions be motivated by them.

Stop and think what one thing you could do today to express appreciation and kindness to someone close to you – then do it!

---

[1] See Col 1:9,10 [2] Luke 2:40 [3] Luke 2:52, NRSV; cf Prov 3:4

BIBLE IN A YEAR: **Genesis 9–11; Acts 4**

Generation to Generation

'... we your people, the sheep of your pasture, will praise you for ever; from generation to generation we will proclaim your praise.'[1]

In the spring of 2022, I completed a multi-day, long-distance walk from Manchester to Exeter. I walked 350 miles in 28 wonderful days. It was not an ordeal but a joy and a pleasure. I walked in the paths created by others. On roads, railway routes, canal towpaths, woolpack trails, pilgrim ways and footpaths, I retraced the steps of workers, walkers and travellers of the years gone by to find my way through valleys and hills to my destination. Proverbs 1–9 says our route through life is similar. Scripture (particularly the book of Proverbs) is our map; wisdom is the path. That path has been made by others who lived before us. It is our task to learn it, walk it and tell of it. It is a tradition passed on from one generation to the next.

Tradition is not much praised these days. This is, in part, because we have discovered much to criticise and avoid in too many of our inherited institutions, practices and behaviours. However, that is not to say that everything is worthless in the traditions we have received. It is now increasingly recognised that tradition is essential to innovation. Far from being its enemy, tradition is a vital creative partner to innovation. The writer of Proverbs seems to know this. He invites readers to face backwards and forwards at the same time; to imbibe the tradition from our parents, grandparents and forebears of the faith and also to care deeply about the next generation and to act generatively on its behalf.

The old ways are not all bad ways. Proverbs invites us to drink deeply from the wells of our faith tradition. It encourages us to draw on the work of those who have gone before us to help us build a theological outlook for the challenges ahead.

Churches are sometimes excellent environments for intergenerational conversation. Talk to someone from a different generation from your own and listen carefully to their story.

[1] Ps 79:13

BIBLE IN A YEAR: **Genesis 12,13; Acts 5**

Just Listen to Yourself!

'May the words of my mouth and the meditation of my heart be acceptable in your sight, O LORD, my Rock and my Redeemer!'[1]

Sometimes our words, or our prayers, give us away. We say something that sounds right on the surface but that reveals a deeper and perhaps unrecognised truth about ourselves. 'I am for peace' cries the psalmist in prayer, 'but ... they are for war' (v 7). Yet similar words are sometimes found on the lips of warmongering aggressors! Nor does it sound like the psalmist is all that much on the side of peace. He seems somewhat gleeful as he makes his imagined address to those he perceives to be liars: 'He will punish you with a warrior's sharp arrows, with burning coals of the broom bush' (v 4); and 'Woe to me that I dwell in Meshek, that I live among the tents of Kedar! Too long have I lived among those who hate peace' (vs 5,6).

Of course, the psalmist's assessment may be entirely accurate, but once we have decided that our neighbours hate peace, there is not much room for negotiation. Once we have concluded that we are right and they are wrong, there is little space for manoeuvre. Though others may share the blame for the conflicts and tensions in which we find ourselves, often we also play a part in creating the problem.

Yet, the words of the psalm are offered to the Lord and this, perhaps, is a saving grace. For prayer provides opportunity not only for making requests but also for listening to our own petitions and learning about ourselves. The half-truths and untruths we tell ourselves are exposed to us when we express them to God in prayer. Thus, we may begin to recognise them for what they are and start to face up to them. The very act of prayer may be a significant step towards peace, despite our enemy and despite ourselves.

Is there someone you are not getting along with? Name them before God and pray that God will bless them, then see whether it makes any difference.

---

[1] Cf Ps 19:14

BIBLE IN A YEAR: **Genesis 14,15; Psalms 3,4**

Tending Your Own Garden

With you, O Lord, is the fountain of life; in your light we see light.[1]

There are numerous passages in Proverbs 1–9 that deal with the 'adulterous woman' (NIV), 'the loose woman' (NRSV) or the 'forbidden woman' (NJPS). This *isha zara* (Hebrew) is an imagined character, or caricature, of whom the young male addressee of Proverbs 1–9 is taught to be wary. This should not, of course, be taken to suggest that women are to be blamed for the sexual misdeeds of men.

Elsewhere, Proverbs presents a more positive portrayal of women than the *isha zara* passages. Indeed, Wisdom itself, the main positive concept of the book, is expressed in grammatically feminine forms and is personified as a woman in the lengthy treatise of chapter 8 and the first few verses of chapter 9. The book also allocates to mothers an important role in the education of the next generation.

Furthermore, Proverbs 31 portrays the 'wife of noble character' as an astute and accomplished leading figure.

Do Proverbs 5 and the other passages featuring the adulterous woman have anything to say to men, women or youths who might read it today? Of course, they do! For it is undeniable that illicit sexual encounters continue to attract both men and women and that sexual temptation continues to exercise a strong force in our world today. Proverbs 5 offers at least two approaches for countering such sexual temptation. First, it exhorts the reader to think about the longer-term outcome of illicit momentary pleasures. Then, it promotes paying attention to one's own home, family, relationships and soul, with the intention that each of us might foster a quality of well-being from which we are unlikely to stray.

Does your manner of life promote health and well-being for yourself and your loved ones? If not, reflect on the changes you need to make.

---

[1] See Ps 36:9

BIBLE IN A YEAR: **Genesis 16,17; Acts 6**

Own Worst Enemy!

'Through many dangers, toils and snares, / I have already come; / 'tis grace has brought me safe thus far, / and grace will lead me home.'[1]

Wisdom is the positive quality feted by the book of Proverbs. Its negative counterpart is folly or foolishness. This is not quite the same as silliness or stupidity, nor does it have much to do with a lack of mental capacity or acuity. Indeed, from the standpoint of Proverbs, you could have the world's greatest scientific mind and still be a fool.

In fact, there is a sliding scale of foolishness in Proverbs, a continuum that describes different classes of fool. At the one end are the young and naive, the very class of people addressed directly by the text. At the other are the recalcitrant and stubbornly wicked, who are characterised by cynical mockery and wilful disregard of all that is good. Proverbs sees the extreme kind of fool as beyond the range of redemption. Such fools are set in their ways and unable to turn and do right. All this sounds pretty grim, except that the stubborn, wayward fool is really a word picture against which the readers, whether young and naive or growing in wisdom, can measure themselves. Proverbs is not really intended for the extreme fool but rather is addressed to impressionable readers, that they might heed the warnings. Even here in chapter 6, which addresses the sluggard, the words are meant for one who is not yet a sluggard: 'Don't be lazy' is the simple message.

The outcome of folly is always harm, whether to fools themselves or to the community at large. In its warnings against folly, Proverbs is asking its readers what kind of footprint they want to leave behind: 'Will you live in such a way as to harm yourself and others, or will you live wisely, carefully and generously, that others will wish to follow in your footsteps?'

Are you making lifestyle choices that are proving harmful to you or to others? Pray, talk to a friend, or find professional help to support you in making some changes.

---

[1] John Newton, 1725–1807, 'Amazing grace!'

BIBLE IN A YEAR: **Genesis 18,19; Acts 7**

Catch the Drama!

'My foes are ever near me, / around me and within; / but, Jesus, draw thou nearer, / and shield my soul from sin.'[1]

A woman in her eighties recently told me she did not much like Proverbs 1–9: 'It's all about sex and young men's temptations. It is not relevant to me.' Proverbs 7 may seem particularly vulnerable to such criticism, for the chapter is a dramatic narrative poem that depicts the seduction of a young man by a brazen adulteress. If universalised, the theme could be misinterpreted to suggest, erroneously, that women are generally seductive or malevolent, or that they are the cause of men's failings.

Whether for purposes of entertainment or education, a drama presents the reader or viewer with a scene or story. This happens in Proverbs 7. Like any TV series, theatre production, movie or novel, the chapter depicts a situation for the reader's imagination. You can almost hear the musical score and the changes in the music as the drama unfolds.

Proverbs 7 might therefore be read as a work of dramatic literature, but it seems to have a deeper purpose. It calls to the young man facing sexual temptation to think about the places he goes, the company he keeps, the situations he puts himself in. Yet it speaks too to any reader. May not any of us be led away or enticed, by others or by our own inclinations, to act in ways that will prove harmful? At the very least, there may be siren voices that distract us from our given task, our commitments or covenant relationships. The passage invites us all to recognise the dangers of distraction or temptation. It invites us to turn to the God of wisdom for the strength and grace we need to live a holy life.

Are you getting too close to someone you shouldn't? Do you need to set firmer boundaries in your life? Find someone you trust and let them help you.

[1] JE Bode, 1816–74, 'O Jesus, I have promised'

BIBLE IN A YEAR: **Genesis 20,21; Acts 8**

Proverbs 8

Like a Playful Child!

'You make known to me the path of life; you will fill me with joy in your presence, with eternal pleasures at your right hand.'[1]

Christians see Jesus in Proverbs 8. They have done so ever since the earliest days of the church. Existing with God before the creation of the world and personified in Proverbs 8, Wisdom begins to sound like the eternal Word made flesh proclaimed in the Gospel of John. Paul may have had this passage in mind when he proclaimed Christ as 'the power of God and the wisdom of God'.[2] This foreshadowing of incarnation is truly wonderful. Yet, I wonder whether the seriousness with which we approach this chapter keeps us from noticing another important aspect: the theme of playfulness!

In verse 30 there is doubt about the best way to understand the Hebrew word sometimes translated 'craftsman' or 'artisan'. At least one early Greek translation understood it to mean 'child'. This is reflected in the NIV footnote and in various translations such as the Revised English Bible: 'Then I was at his side each day, his darling and delight, playing in his presence continually'. Here wisdom is a little child playing by her father's side at the creation of the world. She dances with joy, playing, delighting, rejoicing in all that God is doing. Perhaps Christians might associate Wisdom with the Spirit (also a feminine word in Hebrew), playfully present with the Father and the Word at the creation of the universe.

While the book of Proverbs promotes a strong work ethic and disapproves of laziness, its picture of playful wisdom here confirms what many are learning today: it is wise to play. Play is important, even for adults. It fosters creativity, empathy and well-being, and it aids the learning process. If the wisdom of God incorporates a quality of playfulness, it must follow that those who receive God's wisdom receive an enhanced capacity for play.

If you have children, go and play with them, or play football or tennis, or go for a run or a walk, or play a board game. Just play!

[1] Ps 16:11 [2] 1 Cor 1:24

BIBLE IN A YEAR: **Genesis 22,23; Psalms 5,6**

Cultivating Wisdom

'Teach us to number our days, that we may gain a heart of wisdom.'[1]

A few pages back I mentioned that, in the spring of 2022, I completed a 28-day long, 350-mile walk from Manchester to Exeter. I was walking from our front door to our daughter's front door on a kind of pilgrimage. Although my walk was generally easy, by the end of the very first day and until about the third, everything hurt! The problem was I had set out as if to catch a bus or to reach an engagement in time. My city walking pace was simply too fast for a long walk. How wonderful when I learned to slow down, take in the scene and enjoy the journey! The second problem was that I had set off with too much in my pack and it was weighing me down. At the end of the first day, I had to call on my wife, Dawn, to meet me and relieve me of half its contents. I didn't need all that stuff, I simply had to trust and travel light. The third lesson was that local people knew more than me. New housing was being constructed, a bridge was closed, or a path rerouted and without local knowledge I would have to find out the hard way. At 63 years of age, I had to take up the posture of a nave, simple youth in need of local help and course correction.

Today's passage offers similar lessons both for the journey of life and for navigating through the rest of the book of Proverbs. Wisdom is not attained overnight. It is acquired gradually and only by those who are teachable and open to new learning. Anyone who approaches life – and Proverbs – in this way, will gain much needed help and wisdom for the journey of life.

Read Proverbs 1–9 again. Reflect on your reading. Ask God to help you grow in wisdom. Continue slowly through the rest of the book, one proverb at a time.

[1] Ps 90:12

Scripture Union

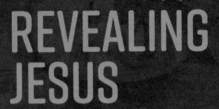

REVEALING
JESUS

FREE:
- COACHING
- AMAZING RESOURCES
- ADVICE & SUPPORT

A flexible and FREE mission framework from Scripture Union

Helping you journey into faith with children and young people who aren't in church.

SU.ORG.UK/REVEALINGJESUS

MISSIONAL ACTS

The Acts of the Apostles is probably the most dramatic and adventurous book in the Bible. Luke composes this story with precise attention to detail and he includes many memorable episodes designed to have an impact on his readers. I have argued elsewhere that Acts is best read as a form of ancient persuasive writing, telling stories from the past to influence readers in their future action.[1] The main theme of the book is mission. Luke tells these vivid stories not merely out of historical interest but to inspire and equip his readers in their own lives and contexts. Reading Acts through this lens illuminates in surprisingly fresh ways many of the stories that Luke tells.

As we walk through striking stories focused on Paul's missionary journeys, we will notice repeated themes, including a focus on: (1) following and being empowered by the Spirit; (2) urban population centres; (3) people of peace and influence; (4) social networks; (5) signs and wonders; (6) relevant preaching; (7) a willingness to suffer; and, above all, (8) the priority of establishing and building the church. These themes shape much of Luke's persuasive missional teaching and their repetition provides helpful clues about what he most wants to communicate to his audience.

As you study this crucial portion of Acts, attempt to read each episode as if for the first time. I'm convinced that overfamiliarity is a significant barrier to receiving their rich message. Luke has written this work to affect his reader profoundly, and the resulting inspiration and provocation is transformative, though not always comfortable. May our eyes be opened to read and engage afresh, and our hearts opened to the Spirit's formation and renovation as we read and study.

Daniel McGinnis

FOR FURTHER READING

My recent book, *Missional Acts*,[1] is a helpful reading companion to Acts, analysing the book from a missional perspective. Craig Keener's commentary on Acts[2] remains the most thorough and detailed commentary. Both sources will inform the background of the following Bible notes.

[1] Daniel McGinnis, *Missional Acts*, Pickwick, 2022 [2] Craig Keener, *Acts: An Exegetical Commentary*, 4 vols, Baker Academic, 2012–2015

A Cauldron of Devotion

'You have made us for yourself, O Lord, and our heart is restless until it finds its rest in you.'[1]

This episode sets the scene for the epic missionary adventures that are to come. For Luke, the church at Antioch plays a crucial missional role. It is the springboard for all of Paul's ensuing journeys, and functions as an ideal model of a sending church. Luke has already emphasised that followers of Jesus are first called Christians here,[2] that it is a large, wealthy and influential congregation[3] and that it is the first place seriously to experiment with multicultural Christian community, including both Jews and non-Jews.[4] Luke then includes a fascinating summary of the diverse Antioch leadership team, which includes Barnabas and Saul (13:1).

This early community is gathered worshipping and fasting (v 2), which provides an important insight into their spiritual fervency. Into this environment of expectant prayer, the Holy Spirit speaks powerfully, leading to Barnabas and Saul being commissioned for God's work. After fasting and praying again, the community lays hands on these two missionaries and sends them off.

This is a crucial turning point in the Acts narrative, for it is the first example of intentional outreach to a location further afield. Up to this point, mission has happened naturally as people have gone about their lives, even while fleeing from persecution, but here we see a new model: a praying church that sends people on missionary journeys. Luke's point is that this emerges out of the cauldron of devotion to God's presence that the church at Antioch has cultivated. This is the pattern in Acts – mission is birthed by a community engaged in ardent prayer, expectant worship and devoted fasting. Today's church longs for the missional effectiveness seen in Acts, but can miss the culture of radical devotion that leads to it.

Could your life be described as a cauldron of devotion to God? How could you help your community cultivate more of this passion for God today?

---

[1] Augustine of Hippo, 354–430, *Confessions*, c397 [2] Acts 11:26 [3] Acts 11:21,24,29,30 [4] Acts 11:20

BIBLE IN A YEAR: **Genesis 26,27; Acts 10**

Reassurance for Pilgrims

'... do not fear, for I am with you; do not be dismayed, for I am your God. I will strengthen you and help you; I will uphold you'.[1]

This psalm is a 'Song of Ascents' – its use as a pilgrimage song provides the key to its meaning. The context is a group of pilgrims making their way up to the Jerusalem Temple to worship at one of the three great religious festivals and lifting their eyes to the surrounding mountains, including Mount Zion. However, it is also relevant to us, to the pilgrimage of Christ's faithful ones towards the future hope that awaits them. The song is composed of four couplets; each has an introductory line, which is then developed over the rest of the couplet.

I remember singing a worship song in my church youth group based on this psalm and thinking that my help comes from the mountains, from some divinity 'up there somewhere'. However, I now understand that the writer is saying the opposite – help does not come from anything dwelling in the mountains, no matter how majestic they are. This may be a subtle reference to idolatry, which often happened in the high places. No, 'My help comes from the LORD, the Maker of heaven and earth' (v 2). This is the psalm's central truth, which is then developed in several ways.

The rest of Psalm 121 is a litany of protection promises – the Lord will not let your foot slip, for he never sleeps (unlike the pagan god Baal); the Lord watches over you and will keep you from all harm, both now and for evermore. These beautiful promises are true for God's people: no matter how treacherous or slippery the way may be, God is with us, watching over us, and we can put our unfaltering trust in his unfailing protection. This is a great comfort when we pass through traumatic experiences. Let's be honest – life is sometimes scary.

In hard times, we need the truths of Psalm 121 more than ever. Read it out loud, slowly, claiming each line as a personal promise for your pilgrimage through life.

[1] Isa 41:10

BIBLE IN A YEAR: **Genesis 28,29; Psalms 7,8**

Acts 13:4–12

Cypriot Fruit

'My message and my preaching were not with wise and persuasive words, but with a demonstration of the Spirit's power, so that your faith might ... rest on ... God's power.'[1]

As Barnabas and Saul are sent out on mission from Antioch, Luke emphasises again that this is the Spirit's work – they are 'sent ... by the Holy Spirit' (v 4). After going through Antioch's seaport Seleucia, they set sail for the island of Cyprus. This prompts the question – why Cyprus? It seems that they don't have a master plan at this point, for there is really no precedent for this sort of missionary journey. I can imagine Saul saying that he has already spent quite a lot of time in his hometown of Tarsus, at which point Barnabas suggests that they go to his home region of Cyprus.[2] His cousin John Mark,[3] also with family in Cyprus, is with them (v 5), so this is actually a logical starting point.

Following family networks and relational attachments, they proclaim the word of God in the Jewish synagogue in Salamis and then make their way across the island to Paphos. Here they encounter an important proconsul (the leader of a Roman senatorial province) named Sergius Paulus. The dramatic confrontation with his attendant Elymas, which results in temporary blindness, leads to Sergius Paulus' faith in Jesus, 'for he was amazed at the teaching about the Lord' (v 12).

This early story establishes multiple missional themes – following the Spirit, social networks, signs and wonders, preaching to receptive audiences, urban centres and a person of influence all play prominent roles. Luke does not say what happens beyond Sergius Paulus' conversion, but the implication is that the faith of such an influential person within the entire region will ensure the continued spread of the word throughout Cyprus.

Arguments and apologetics only go so far – what transforms people is experience of the power and love of God. How can you give people this opportunity to encounter Jesus today?

---

[1] 1 Cor 2:4,5 [2] Acts 4:36,37 [3] Col 4:10

BIBLE IN A YEAR: **Genesis 30,31; Acts 11**

Pertinent Pisidian Preaching

'Don't you have a saying, "It's still four months until harvest"? I tell you, open your eyes and look at the fields! They are ripe for harvest.'[1]

Paul and his companions depart Paphos and travel to Pisidian Antioch, where Paul's first major speech takes place. This is another Antioch, in the region of Pisidia; in fact, there are at least fifteen cities named Antioch in the empire, mostly named after Antiochus, king of Syria after the death of Alexander the Great. But why Pisidian Antioch? Interestingly, scholars have found inscriptions indicating that Sergius Paulus was from there originally and it could be that he urged them to go and share the good news with his relatives. If so, this again hints at the role social networks play behind the scenes in Paul's travel choices.

They again go first to the synagogue – this is a logical strategy, for they are received as travelling Jewish teachers and provided with a receptive audience (v 15). Paul begins by addressing two groups: his Jewish hearers and 'Gentiles who worship God' (v 16). This second group, commonly known as 'God-fearers', are not full Jewish converts but synagogue adherents on the fringes of the Jewish community. They are a frequent narrative theme in Acts and are often Paul's most receptive audience, for they are drawn to his message because it shares Jewish Scripture, theology and ethics, but lacks the cultural requirements for full conversion, such as circumcision and dietary requirements.

Paul goes on to provide a masterclass in contextual preaching, filled with allusions to the Hebrew Scriptures. He begins with a sweep of biblical history, clearly wanting his hearers to understand that his message is not based on isolated proof texts but on the whole pattern of God's working throughout history. Paul delivers a thoroughly Jewish speech, crafting his case for Christ from scripture that is relevant and authoritative to his synagogue listeners.

You may not have a natural audience like Paul – but who in your life is receptive to the gospel? How can you talk of Christ so that they may hear?

---

[1] John 4:35

BIBLE IN A YEAR: **Genesis 32,33; Acts 12**

Acts 13:26–41

A Bold Appeal to Respond

'After they prayed, the place where they were meeting was shaken. And they were all filled with the Holy Spirit and spoke the word of God boldly.'[1]

After his summary of Jewish biblical history, Paul goes on to focus more on Christ and the message of salvation in this portion of his Pisidian Antioch synagogue speech. However, he continues to preach in a thoroughly Jewish way, lacing his speech with references to the familiar figures of Abraham, Moses, David, the prophets and Israel itself. Towards the end, he quotes four Old Testament passages (vs 33–41).[2] These have a messianic thrust and focus on the reality of the resurrection, which seems to be the crux of Paul's salvation message. Paul emphasises the prophetic fulfilment of the Christ event: 'what God promised our ancestors he has fulfilled for us, their children, by raising up Jesus' (vs 32,33).

Paul is building affinity with his hearers by speaking as a Jewish insider, as one of them, yet he is not afraid to confront them. After tying his Christological message as convincingly as possible into the Jewish scriptural worldview and framework, he declares that, because Jesus has been raised from the dead, believers are 'set free from every sin, a justification you were not able to obtain under the law of Moses' (v 39). He finishes with a solemn warning against unbelief, quoting Habakkuk about scoffers who will perish.

This is no tame speech! Paul offers forgiveness of sins through Jesus, in a masterfully crafted Jewish speech, full of rhetorical flourishes which establish rapport and common ground. Yet he does not let his hearers off the hook – they must respond to this news, one way or another. He presses them for a reaction to the good news about Jesus.

We may feel cultural pressures about how we speak about Christ today. Luke, however, encourages us to follow Paul's example in boldly asking our hearers to respond to the gospel.

[1] Acts 4:31 [2] Ps 2:7; Isa 55:3; Ps 16:10; Hab 1:5

BIBLE IN A YEAR: **Genesis 34–36; Acts 13**

Aim for Higher Impact

Loving Father, please give us God-sized dreams to dream and the faith to partner with you in seeing them come to pass, in the mighty name of Jesus.

When Paul returns to speak on the next Sabbath, some Jews incite the crowds to turn against him, causing him to turn to the Gentiles. This develops Luke's theme that everyone is welcome in the Jesus movement, regardless of ethnicity, geography, gender, social status or anything else. The Old Testament quotation also functions as a 'proof from prophecy', validating the divine legitimacy and necessity of the Gentile mission. Luke is revealing his conviction that God's mission is for everyone, Jew and Gentile alike, and that this was God's plan from the beginning.

Gentiles believe in Christ as a result of Paul's invitation, and a new church is born in Pisidian Antioch (v 48). Luke then says, 'The word of the Lord spread [or was carried] through the whole region' (v 49). Luke is implying that messengers carry the word throughout the whole region that Antioch controls. Luke makes no claim that Paul is directly involved in this wider outreach, instead reporting his quick expulsion from the city (vs 50,51). This highlights a vital missional strategy. Paul establishes the initial nucleus of believers, only staying long enough to establish foundations of faith and mission.

We can assume that local missionaries with their own social networks and credibility (which Paul lacks), drawn from the recently established churches, carry out this regional mission. Paul begins this process and probably has a role in training them, but the implication is that local believers are empowered and mobilised to take responsibility for outreach in their surrounding areas, initiating a reproducing strategy of growth capable of impacting large areas relatively quickly (v 49).

Christians impacting their region is the repeated pattern in Acts: Jerusalem, Judea, Samaria and the ends of the earth.[1] Lord, expand our faith, empower us by your Spirit.

[1] Acts 1:8

BIBLE IN A YEAR: **Genesis 37,38; Psalm 9**

Acts 14:1–7

Signs that Lead to Wonder

'Stretch out your hand to heal and perform signs and wonders through the name of your holy servant Jesus.'[1]

Paul and Barnabas flee to Iconium after being expelled from the region of Pisidian Antioch. This is a journey of at least 90 miles, on the *Via Sebaste*, a broad and well-paved road connecting local Roman colonies. As is his modus operandi, Paul uses the best travel routes and stops in the next city that has a synagogue.

Paul and Barnabas speak boldly in Iconium for a 'considerable time' (v 3). Luke adds that the Lord 'confirmed the message of his grace by enabling them to perform signs and wonders'. The Greek word for sign means a distinguishing mark whereby something is known, or a confirmation. The word for wonder means something that astounds because of its transcendent associations, such as an omen or portent. These concepts summarise the role of the miraculous in the mission: it confirms the message being preached and causes people to wonder in astonishment (this is confirmed in 15:12 before the Jerusalem Council).

Luke is not interested in miracles for their own sake, but in miracles that confirm the truthfulness of the word being proclaimed and make people wonder what power is behind it. I remember praying for someone with severe scoliosis who was dramatically healed as they responded to the good news about God's love, while on a mission trip in Mexico as a student. It was astonishing to watch a back shaped like an 'S' become totally straight! This and many other personal experiences have convinced me that God is still doing the sorts of miraculous things described in Acts, just as he has throughout church history. Signs and wonders still authenticate the gospel message today.

God may not heal everyone we pray for in the way we expect. But God still works miracles that cause people to wonder. Give him that opportunity by praying faithfully.

---

[1] Acts 4:30

BIBLE IN A YEAR: **Genesis 39,40; Acts 14**

Acts 14:8-20

Suffering and Sovereignty

'The apostles left the Sanhedrin, rejoicing because they had been counted worthy of suffering disgrace for the Name.'[1]

Paul and Barnabas flee persecution in Iconium and arrive in Lystra, where a lame man is healed, leading to a brief gospel proclamation. This message is noticeably different from the synagogue message in Pisidian Antioch: there is no mention of Jews or a synagogue in Lystra, so they seek to find common ground with a Gentile audience through natural theology, without even a mention of the Hebrew Scriptures (vs 14–18). Once again, we see how Paul, an expert rhetorician, feels free to contextualise his message about Jesus to be relevant to his audience.

Paul's interaction with the Lystrans takes a violent turn when Jews from Pisidian Antioch and Iconium arrive and convince the crowds to stone him, drag him out of the city and leave him for dead. Paul attracts riots and public disorder like a magnet throughout Acts, but this incident is one of the most serious, for his life is clearly in danger. Luke emphasises that this is sometimes the result when one takes the mission of God seriously. Early Christians considered suffering for Christ to be an honour. Luke reassures his readers that they should not be surprised when they suffer, but should trust that God will care for them, as he cares for Paul.

The Lystran disciples gather around Paul, presumably in prayer and for his protection, and the next day Paul leaves for Derbe, where he experiences further missional success. The way Luke recounts these episodes emphasises God's sovereignty – human opposition can never defeat the mission, for divine providence sustains and furthers it. There seems to be plenty of room in the theological worldview of the early church for suffering, alongside a conviction that God is bigger and will use it for his glory, however painful it may be.

Do you regard suffering for Christ to be an honour? Nobody wants suffering, but stories like this can help us to be prepared, trusting God when it comes our way.

[1] Acts 5:41

BIBLE IN A YEAR: **Genesis 41,42; Acts 15**

Psalm 122

Holistic Flourishing

'You will keep in perfect peace [*shalom shalom* – complete wholeness, fullness of flourishing] those whose minds are steadfast, because they trust in you.'[1]

This is another 'Song of Ascents', part of a wider grouping of 15 other such psalms (120–134). As with Psalm 121, this song evokes images of a pilgrim arriving in Jerusalem, probably for one of the three annual festivals.[2] The psalmist rejoices over Jerusalem, acknowledges the significance of the Temple as 'the house of the LORD' (v 1) and prays for the peace of Jerusalem.

The dominant theme of the final four verses is a prayer for 'peace'. This word is *shalom*, which means much more than the absence of conflict. *Shalom* is a rich concept, suggesting completeness, justice, health, well-being and protection. The world cannot provide this kind of *shalom* – such deep wholeness can only come from God. 'Holistic flourishing' is a helpful summary, for it applies to every aspect of life, including our inner life and outward relationships, speaking of an integrated wholeness and fullness. This beautiful idea is emphasised repeatedly in verses 6 to 8. Verse 6 contains a stunning Hebrew wordplay of four straight words, all of which have the core *shalu* or *shalom* sound: 'Pray for (*shalu*) the peace (*shalom*) of Jerusalem (*yerushalam*), may they prosper (*yishalu*) who love you.' These concepts, which include security and prosperity, are tightly bound together in this poetic Hebrew wordplay.

Every New Year I ask God for a 'word for the year', which often becomes a helpful focus for me. This year I felt God speak 'Shalom' to me, so I've been studying this rich Hebrew concept. One of my favourite promises is 'Great peace [*Shalom*, holistic flourishing] have those who love your law, and nothing can make them stumble.'[3] It's been a turbulent few years for my family, with multiple serious health struggles, and this truth has been a much-needed refuge in troubled times.

To find peace of mind and peace with others, we must first find peace with and in God; then nothing will cause us to stumble.

---

[1] Isa 26:3 [2] Deut 16:16 [3] Ps 119:165

BIBLE IN A YEAR: **Genesis 43,44; Psalm 10**

Strategic Strengthening

'Now you are the body of Christ, and each one of you is a part of it.'[1]
Lord Jesus, give us your loving heart for your church.

It would have been much easier for Paul and Barnabas to continue to Syrian Antioch overland via Tarsus, the city of Paul's birth. Instead they take the long road back, through all the cities they have just visited. Their reason is clear – this is a pastoral visitation of each new church. Luke says they were 'strengthening the disciples and encouraging them to remain true to the faith' (v 22). The verb 'strengthen' is only found in Acts: Luke uses it four times to underscore its strategic significance, all in the context of strengthening fellow believers.[2]

The visiting of existing churches represents a new stage in Paul's missional strategy. After the founding of the core of a Christian community, he tends to leave quickly, often forced out by threats and persecution. He wants to prevent these new churches from growing overly dependent on him, allowing them to learn how to function independently. However, he does not leave them permanently, but returns for pastoral visits to train and strengthen them in their faith and mission. We know from his many letters that writing is another strategy with a similar goal. Galatians is probably written to these very churches in Iconium, Lystra and Pisidian Antioch.

In addition to strengthening and encouraging these infant churches, Paul appoints 'elders' (v 23) for each new congregation. This results in a long-term, local leadership structure, which will help them to develop in a healthy way. It allows local leaders to emerge and provide the pastoral care these churches require and supplies the young communities with much-needed stability, sustainability and direction for further missional growth.

Paul's top priority is always the church. What can you do to build up and strengthen your spiritual community? Pray for creative ideas to strengthen believers around you today.

---

[1] 1 Cor 12:27 [2] Acts 14:22; 15:32; 15:41; 18:23

BIBLE IN A YEAR: **Genesis 45,46; Acts 16**

Acts 15:1–11

How Sweet the Sound

'... since we have been justified through faith, we have peace with God through our Lord Jesus Christ, through whom we have gained access by faith into this grace'.[1]

It is difficult to comprehend the seismic shift the inclusion of Gentiles brings about in the early church. Up to this point, the church has essentially been a Jewish phenomenon. However, the Ethiopian eunuch, Cornelius' conversion and the Antioch church all hint at God's broader inclusive agenda. This becomes the norm in the Pauline churches, for the most responsive converts tend to be the Gentiles whom Paul encounters. This prompts a genuine crisis in the early church: the Jerusalem Council of Acts 15 is the leadership's attempt to address this.

The crux of the issue is the role of the Jewish Law in salvation. How much should the Law's requirements, including circumcision, apply to these new Gentile converts, who have no other Jewish affiliation (v 5)? The question is not whether non-Jews should be included, but on what basis. This passionate debate becomes the main factor prompting the widening separation between Christianity and Judaism. In the initial discussion, Peter reminds them that the Spirit clearly showed God's acceptance of Gentiles by coming upon Cornelius and his household dramatically when they believed.

He then gives a profound summary: 'why do you try to test God by putting on the necks of Gentiles a yoke that neither we nor our ancestors have been able to bear? No! We believe it is through the grace of our Lord Jesus that we are saved, just as they are' (vs 10,11). Peter sets out his firm belief that nobody can actually fulfil the Law. Not just Gentiles, but Jews as well, are saved through God's grace alone.[2] This dramatically levels the playing field – all stand before God equally in need of grace.

This is the good news – because of the cross, you stand forgiven and cleansed by grace. Take time now to simply give thanks.

---

[1] Rom 5:1,2 [2] Cf Rom 3:9

BIBLE IN A YEAR: **Genesis 47,48; Acts 17**

Fight for Unity

'How good and pleasant it is when God's people live together in unity! It is like precious oil poured on the head, running down on the beard'.[1]

It is both sobering and somehow reassuring to recognise that even in the earliest days of the Christian movement there was conflict, debate and contention. The church has rarely managed to avoid such divisions since then, and the current radical splintering and disunity of the church is perhaps modern Christianity's greatest tragedy. Acts is honest about division in the earliest church, but also presents models for how to resolve such conflicts,[2] which could prove helpful today.

The Jerusalem council provides a number of important steps that early believers took to resolve the painful conflict between the Antioch and Jerusalem churches: (1) the Antioch church proactively sends a delegation to pursue a resolution to the pressing problem (vs 1–3); (2) these delegates meet face to face with the Jerusalem leaders to give their report and set another time to continue the discussion (vs 4–6); (3) both sides are given time to present their views, with a focus on the testimonies of what God has recently done through Paul and Barnabas, prompting the current crisis (vs 5–12); (4) James, the primary Jerusalem leader, summarises the reports and presents a compromise solution, thoroughly based on Scripture (vs 13–21); (5) this placates both sides, and everyone agrees to abide by the decision (vs 22,28); (6) the council sends a delegation of members of both parties to Antioch to report the decision (vs 22–30); and (7) the fruit of this new-found unity is encouragement, peace and further ministry (vs 31–35).

Problems in the church must be confronted. All sides of the argument must be given a fair hearing. Leaders who are spiritually mature and trustworthy can then make wise decisions that lead to life and growth.

The church should follow this example and preserve relational unity. As far as it depends on you, commit to following God's leadership in conflict resolution.

[1] Ps 133:1,2 [2] Eg Acts 6:1–7

BIBLE IN A YEAR: **Genesis 49,50; Acts 18**

Acts 15:22–35

Multicultural Beauty

'… so that they may be brought to complete unity. Then the world will know that you sent me and have loved them even as you have loved me.'[1]

Jews and Gentiles had so little in common in the ancient world – different histories, cultures, customs, practices, traditions, even languages. The early church faced the immense difficulty of bringing such diverse peoples together. One option is always to segregate, isolate and regard each other with suspicion. This all-too-common response has greatly hindered Christianity's missional effectiveness. When division or judgementalism prevails, the church betrays Christ's teaching and loses its appeal.

The other solution is to surrender our prejudices and presuppositions to the greater purposes of God and allow him to shape us and remove the barriers to unity. Imitating Christ means becoming tolerant, understanding and accepting of the other, the different, the excluded. Nothing gives God greater glory or provides a more compelling witness than when believers of different ethnicities, backgrounds and social status come together in love to worship Jesus.

At this great crossroads in the life of the church in Acts, we see a lived example of this. All sides are represented, not just in the resolution itself but also in the party that returns to Antioch to bring the news (v 22). The decision itself contains important compromise on both sides. The Gentiles do not need to be circumcised or follow the Law, but they are asked to follow four stipulations, each of which is particularly important to devout Jews. This negotiated and creative resolution allows the church to grow in unity and remain unhindered by entrenched cultural differences. The direct result is encouragement, strengthening, unity, peace and further outreach (vs 30–35).

Have you a vision of a multicultural church, learning to live in community? Can you be more inclusive, letting Christ lead you in surrendering your prejudices and embracing the other?

[1] John 17:23

BIBLE IN A YEAR: **Exodus 1,2; Psalms 11,12**

Painful Disagreements

'Lord, make me an instrument of your peace. Where there is hatred, let me sow love; where there is injury, pardon'.[1]

I have already mentioned that I appreciate Luke's honesty in portraying the problems of the early church. This episode contains a shocking example. The godly heroes of this portion of the narrative, Luke's archetypal missionaries, who have seemingly spread the church more widely than anyone else, come to a painful separation. In fact, Luke describes Paul and Barnabas having a 'sharp disagreement' (v 39). This is an extremely strong Greek word, implying a provocation or angry dispute. The dispute is about whether to take John Mark with them again, as he 'deserted' them during their previous missionary journey (v 38). It is so vehement that they separate and go their own ways.

If extremely godly men such as Paul and Barnabas, who are clearly led by the Spirit and wholehearted in their devotion to Christ, can have such a vehement disagreement, what hope is there for the rest of us? Or, looked at another way, if leaders like these can have such a conflict, perhaps this gives hope for the rest of us. This episode speaks to the inevitability of occasional relationship breakdown, yet its resolution should give us hope.

This is the last we hear of either Barnabas or Mark in Acts. However, it is not the end of the story. Various hints in Paul's letters show his enduring respect for Barnabas.[2] Mark, too, is later included in Paul's group[3] and Paul comes to admire him so much that he requests his presence in his final days, describing him as 'helpful to me in my ministry'.[4] A painful disagreement has clearly been overcome and unity of relationship has been restored. Restored relationships are often stronger and deeper than they were before the dispute.

Conflicts are inevitable in community, but it matters how we handle them and how we pursue reconciliation. Ask God to make you a bridge-builder.

[1] Francis of Assisi, c1181–1226 [2] 1 Cor 9:6; Gal 2:11–13 [3] Col 4:10; Phlm 24 [4] 2 Tim 4:11

BIBLE IN A YEAR: **Exodus 3,4; Acts 19**

A Person of Influence

'So I say to you: ask and it will be given to you; seek and you will find; knock and the door will be opened to you.'[1]

When Paul and Barnabas part ways, Paul takes Silas and Timothy with him on his second missionary journey. After a dramatic summons to Macedonia, they follow the Spirit's guidance and arrive in Philippi. There is apparently not a sufficient Jewish population in the city for a synagogue, so Paul goes outside the gates to the Jewish 'place of prayer' by the river (v 13). Here he meets Lydia, a dealer in purple cloth from Thyatira. Lydia is a crucial person of peace[2] and becomes a strategic gateway for Paul into Philippi.

We can note the characteristics that make Lydia an ideal person of influence. She is a God-fearer with cultural and religious common ground with Paul, providing natural rapport and points of connection (vs 13,14). She is a householder, so Paul, by reaching Lydia, reaches into the power-centre of an entire household network (v 15). She is spiritually interested and 'opened her heart' (v 14) in response to the Lord's initiative. Lydia's friendships, social status and business contacts provide a social base for outreach. Her reputation and influence in the community provide Paul and his message with social credibility (v 14). She provides hospitality during Paul's stay, her house a physical base for mission and a home for the new church in Philippi (vs 15,40). Finally, Lydia's relative wealth offers a financial base for outreach in Philippi and the wider region (vs 14,40).

Luke consistently highlights people of relatively high status and means who play a strategic role in the birth and growth of the Pauline churches. This does not mean that Paul overlooks the poor and needy, but it is Luke's rhetorical way of advocating this specific missional strategy.

How might God be inviting you to be more strategic in your missional efforts? What influential gatekeepers (like Lydia) do you know?

---

[1] Luke 11:9 [2] Cf Luke 10:5–7

BIBLE IN A YEAR: **Exodus 5,6; Acts 20**

Dependency and Confidence

'Trust the past to the mercy of God, the present to his love, and the future to his providence.'[1]

Today's psalm has a simple structure: the introduction in verse 1 is followed by two brief stanzas, each developing its own motif. The overarching theme is looking to God for mercy in total dependency, while enduring painful reproach from enemies. The psalmist speaks as a representative or spokesperson of the whole community – note the change from the first person singular, 'I', in verse 1 to 'our' and 'we' in the rest of the psalm.

The psalmist uses two vivid similes drawn from domestic life in verse 2: a male slave and a female servant or maid. Both are looking to their master, in hope of mercy. While such imagery may sit somewhat uncomfortably with modern readers, this is a common situation in the ancient world. The author's point seems to be to emphasise the total reliance God's people have on him and to encourage his readers to wait in utter dependence upon God.

Reading this psalm in the light of the cross and resurrection, we can jubilantly declare that God has answered the psalmist's plea and poured out his mercy lavishly through Christ. We are still thoroughly dependent upon God's mercy yet, because of what Christ has done, we stand justified before him. We can approach his throne of grace with confidence, that we may receive mercy and find grace to help us in our time of need.[2] This combination of total dependency and absolute confidence is the unique privilege of followers of Christ. It is also the ideal springboard for spiritual growth. We acknowledge with the psalmist our utter need for God, and yet rejoice that his mercy has been extravagantly poured out. The only reasonable response is grateful service.

Apply this great reality to the challenges and heartaches of your life. Read the psalm aloud, asking God for his mercy in your particular circumstances and thanking him for Jesus.

[1] Attributed to Augustine of Hippo, 354–430 [2] Heb 4:16

BIBLE IN A YEAR: **Exodus 7,8; Psalms 13,14**

Willing to Suffer

'Whoever wants to be my disciple must deny themselves and take up their cross daily and follow me.'[1]

Paul continues his outreach in Philippi, growing the new church based in Lydia's household. In this process he encounters a fortune-telling slave girl with a 'python spirit' (v 16, in some translations), a reference to the serpent or dragon that guarded the famous Delphic oracle at Mount Parnassus. Paul becomes so annoyed that he eventually commands the spirit to come out of her in the name of Jesus. This unusual story contributes to one of Luke's favourite themes: nothing can hinder the gospel, not even a powerful demonic spirit. It is one of a series of dramatic power encounters in Acts, all of which emphasise this important theological point about the supremacy of the Christian God.

Paul's mission often damages the fortunes of pagan worshippers and craftsmen (as in Ephesus[2]). Here, the owners of the slave girl who have lost their ability to make money have Paul and Silas arrested and placed in custody. The two undergo a painful litany of punishments: they are stripped, severely flogged with rods[3] and locked in the inner cell of the local jail, with stocks around their feet. These stocks are painful wooden restraints placed around the ankles, used not just for security, but also for torture.

Once again, we see Paul suffering violence and injustice on behalf of the gospel. It seems that he has connected suffering with proclamation and Luke presents this as the expected result of the mission. Paul teaches the new disciples in his churches, 'We must go through many hardships to enter the kingdom of God'[4] and he regularly models this. Acts is not triumphalistic: though the gospel is triumphant, its bearers must walk the way of the cross, the way of suffering.

Following Jesus is costly: taking up our cross really hurts sometimes. Are you willing to suffer as you carry your cross, trusting Jesus? Ask God for grace to say 'Yes'.

---

[1] Luke 9:23 [2] Acts 19:23–41 [3] Cf 2 Cor 11:25 [4] Acts 14:22

BIBLE IN A YEAR: **Exodus 9,10; Acts 21**

Sacrificial Devotion

'My grace is sufficient for you, for my power is made perfect in weakness.'[1] Thank you, Lord.

Amid painful suffering and imprisonment, the response from Paul and Silas is remarkable: 'About midnight Paul and Silas were praying and singing hymns to God' (v 25). Once again, their willingness to suffer advances the mission. Their spiritual devotion sustains them through danger and pain. They know that God has providentially led them to Philippi (vs 9,10) and it may be that they worship God now not simply despite their sufferings but even *for* their sufferings. They are living Paul's challenging advice, by '*always* giving thanks to God the Father *for everything*, in the name of our Lord Jesus Christ.'[2]

Luke adds a missional dimension to their exuberant worship by noting that 'the other prisoners were listening to them' (v 25). You can imagine how bizarre this must have seemed in an environment of such fear and danger! God responds to their devotion with an earthquake, which spectacularly releases them from their captivity. This is another example of the miraculous confirmation of Paul's message.[3] The jailer certainly interprets the earthquake this way. After almost killing himself in despair and being reassured that his prisoners have not fled, he rushes in and cries out, 'what must I do to be saved?' (v 30). The ensuing salvation of his entire household is a further triumph for the gospel that Paul and Silas proclaim, both in their words and in their vivid example of sacrificial devotion.

Paul and Silas are Roman citizens – a major embarrassment for the local authorities, who ask them to leave the city. They don't leave immediately, however. Their first priority is to strengthen and encourage the new Philippian church meeting in Lydia's home.

Paul's sacrificial devotion in the face of suffering led to dramatic missional breakthrough. How can you emulate this in your own life? Receive God's all-sufficient grace in your weakness.

---

[1] 2 Cor 12:9 [2] Eph 5:20, italics added [3] Cf 2 Cor 12:12

BIBLE IN A YEAR: **Exodus 11,12; Acts 22**

Connecting You with all God's doing through Scripture Union

Subscribe to *Connecting You* for FREE to get all the latest news and stories from Scripture Union + daily prayer pointers to help fuel your prayers.

A GOD OF FAITHFULNESS

The books of Kings cover more than four hundred years of Israelite history, divided into three sections: the end of David's reign and the reign of Solomon (1 Kings 1–11); the divided monarchy of Israel and Judah (1 Kings 12 – 2 Kings 17); and the kingdom of Judah alone after the fall of Israel (2 Kings 18–25). It is noteworthy that the books are not all about the kings and their times, but rather more about God and loyalty to him.

These coming three weeks focus on 2 Kings 9–25. This section starts with Jehu's rise to power and then records the swirling downfall of Israel after the prime time of Jehu's dynasty. It displays a mixed bag of good and bad kings of Judah, among whom Hezekiah and Josiah are considered to be the best rulers. The destruction of Israel serves as a warning to Judah, but unfortunately Judah follows Israel's fatal path.

As elsewhere in both books of Kings, David is used in 2 Kings 9–25 as a standard for comparison to evaluate the southern kings (eg 14:3; 16:2; 18:3; 22:2).[1] Jeroboam, son of Nebat, is used as a reference point to evaluate the northern kings (eg 9:9; 10:29; 13:2,11; 14:24; 15:9,18,24,28;).[2] However, at some point, the corrupt kings of Judah (Ahaz and Manasseh) are compared with the kings of Israel (16:3; 21:3). Despite the great reforms of Hezekiah and Josiah, the cumulative sins of the nation led to the irreversible disaster in Judah. Amid the totality of the devastation of Judah, the book surprisingly ends on a note of hope (25:27–30), which serves to remind the Jewish exiles of God's promise to David.[3] The lamp of David never vanishes – even on the brink of extinction.

Alison Lo

---

[1] Cf 1 Kings 9:4,5; 11:4,6,38; 14:8; 15:3,11 [2] Cf 1 Kings 16:2,3,26,31; 21:22; 22:52 [3] 2 Sam 7:16; 2 Kings 8:19

2 Kings 9

Divine Retribution

Come, O come, Holy Spirit! / Open our ears to hear your voice. / Open our hearts to understand your word. / Open our mouths to speak your truth.

Elijah was commanded to anoint Jehu as king over Israel,[1] but this task is not accomplished until Elisha appoints a young prophet to fulfil this mission (vs 1–13). God raises up Jehu to revenge the blood of Naboth, who was killed by Ahab for not giving up his vineyard to feed the king's greed because Naboth knew that the Lord forbade him to give away his ancestral inheritance.[2] God had declared the total destruction of Ahab's house,[3] especially Jezebel,[4] who had initiated the evil plot to pervert justice on behalf of Ahab.[5]

The prophecy about Ahab's death had already been fulfilled[6] and now it is Jezebel's turn to face her destiny. After entering the gate of Jezreel, Jehu commands the eunuchs to throw Jezebel out of the window. When they go to bury her, only the skull, the feet and the palms of her hands are found as the dogs have eaten her body (vs 35–37, NRSV), which vividly fulfils the word of the Lord through Elijah.[7]

The divine retaliation for Naboth's innocent death demonstrates that God stands up for the oppressed, powerless and voiceless, even though the earthly king has failed to execute justice. The wickedness of Ahab and Jezebel bears consequences. The result is to bring curses on themselves, the 70 sons of Ahab, anyone related to them and all Baal worshippers, who are to be executed by Jehu.[8] God will certainly repay people for their own sin. Most amazingly, the word of the Lord never fails. The fulfilment of the divine word is repeatedly seen in this chapter (vs 3,6,12,26,36).

If we are saddened by the social injustice around us, may the fate of Ahab and his house remind us of God's sovereignty, unyielding justice and unfailing Word.

---

[1] 1 Kings 19:16 [2] 1 Kings 21:3 [3] 1 Kings 21:17–24 [4] 1 Kings 21:23,24 [5] 1 Kings 21:4–16 [6] 1 Kings 22:37,38 [7] 1 Kings 21:23 [8] 2 Kings 10

BIBLE IN A YEAR: **Exodus 13,14; Acts 23**

Serve God Wholeheartedly

'Search me, God, and know my heart; test me and know my anxious thoughts. See if there is any offensive way in me, and lead me in the way everlasting.'[1]

Jehu's brutality in chapter 9 continues through chapter 10. He orders the slaughter of all 70 sons of Ahab and everyone related to Ahab, leaving him no survivor. Jehu is the only king in the northern kingdom to be commended for executing God's will by eliminating the house of Ahab (v 30) and eradicating Baal worship (v 28). For this reason, God promises that Jehu's descendants will sit on the throne of Israel to the fourth generation (v 30).

Nevertheless, the comments on Jehu are not all positive; the text reveals the limits of his zeal. He doesn't keep the law of God with all his heart, because he never turns away from the sins of Jeroboam, who had caused Israel to worship the golden calves at Bethel and Dan (vs 29,31). This apostasy eventually leads to the reduction of the size of Israel and its being overpowered by neighbouring countries (vs 32,33). Beyond our outward actions, God looks into a person's inner motivation. What God actually requires of us is to obey him with all our hearts. Unfortunately, Jehu falls short of wholeheartedness.

Some people may find it difficult to understand how injustice can be dealt with by violence. Further evaluation on Jehu can be found outside the book of Kings. Far from approving the bloodshed at Jezreel, Hosea makes it clear that the Lord would punish 'the house of Jehu for the massacre at Jezreel'.[2] Throughout human history, God sometimes paradoxically achieves his divine plan through wicked people or evil plots. In all these human flaws, God's sovereignty always triumphs. The story of the cross is the best example.

Lord, examine our hearts, even when we act zealously for you. May we serve you with an upright spirit and pure motives. May our agendas align with your divine will.

[1] Ps 139:23,24 [2] Hos 1:3–5

BIBLE IN A YEAR: **Exodus 15,16; Psalm 15**

2 Kings 11

Make a Difference

'You are the salt of the earth ... You are the light of the world.'[1]

As Jezebel is to Israel, Athaliah is to Judah. After her son Ahaziah was killed by Jehu,[2] Athaliah (the daughter of Ahab and presumably Jezebel) attempts to annihilate David's line in Judah, in order to seize the throne. Jehosheba (Ahaziah's sister) and the priest Jehoiada (Jehosheba's husband) hide infant Joash (Jehoash) son of Ahaziah in the Temple to protect the young prince (vs 1–11).[3]

Jehoiada later crowns seven-year old Joash as king and executes Athaliah. The lamp of David is preserved in Judah, according to God's promise.[4] As with Jezebel, Athaliah's association with Ahab and her wickedness lead to her dreadful death. Jehu caused enormous bloodshed, whereas Jehoiada only puts Athaliah and Mattan to death. Apart from political restoration, the priest renews the covenants between the Lord, the king and people (v 17).

The royal intermarriage with the house of Ahab has led to the prevalent worship of Baal in Judah. Like Jehu, who purged the Baal influence in Israel, Jehoiada destroys Baal's temple, altars and images and kills a Baal priest, Mattan (v 18). Unlike Jehu, however, who failed to follow the law of the Lord with all his heart and never turned away from the sins of Jeroboam,[5] Jehoiada seeks to restore the worship of Yahweh by covenant renewal in Judah (v 17). Jehoiada's acts of restoration are well received by the people in Judah, as shown in verse 20: 'All the people of the land rejoiced, and the city was calm, because Athaliah had been slain with the sword at the palace.' It lays a solid foundation for Joash's reform later on. Amidst all the political turmoil, Jehoiada makes a huge difference in his nation.

How can we make a difference in our own community? Let's listen to the voice of the Holy Spirit and see how he directs us in the coming week.

---

[1] Matt 5:13,14 [2] 2 Kings 9:27 [3] See also 2 Chr 22:11 [4] 2 Kings 8:19 [5] 2 Kings 10:31

BIBLE IN A YEAR: **Exodus 17,18; Acts 24**

Fight the Good Fight

'... so that you may live a life worthy of the Lord and please him in every way: bearing fruit in every good work, growing in the knowledge of God'.[1]

Following the instruction of the priest Jehoiada, King Joash renovates the Temple during his reign in Judah. Though Joash is commended by God, he is criticised for failing to remove the high places, where people continue their pagan worship. Joash summons the priests to collect money from the census taxes and voluntary offerings for the Temple restoration and to oversee the project.[2] Additional donations are collected to pay the repair workers to resume the Temple maintenance, which had been delayed because of a shortage of funds.

Threatened by the Aramaean attack, Joash gives Hazael king of Aram all the Temple treasury dedicated by his predecessors, to buy him off. Ironically, Joash set his mind to restore the Temple, but in the end he robs it. The chapter ends on a tragic note as Joash is murdered by his officials. However, the stripping of the Temple treasury remains undenounced and the assassination of Joash unexplained here. The book of Chronicles, however, points out that Joash does right when Jehoiada is alive and that his reign is marred by covenant failure, idolatry and hostility between Joash and the priests after Jehoiada's death.[3] Zechariah, the son of Jehoiada, publicly rebukes Joash, who thereafter stones the priest to death, after triggering conspiracy against him in the nation.[4] Chronicles remarks that the apostasy of Joash leads to the domination by the Aramaeans and his assassination by his own servants.[5] Just as Joash did, it's often easy to start a work for God with great enthusiasm. To finish well is quite another story.

May Paul's words spur us on: 'I have fought the good fight, I have finished the race, I have kept the faith'.[6]

[1] Col 1:10 [2] Exod 30:11–16; Lev 27:1–8 [3] 2 Chr 24:2,17–22 [4] 2 Chr 24:20–22 [5] 2 Chr 24:23–25 [6] 2 Tim 4:7

BIBLE IN A YEAR: **Exodus 19,20; Acts 25**

Psalm 124

God on Our Side

'He who did not spare his own Son, but gave him up for us all – how will he not also, along with him, graciously give us all things?'[1]

The previous psalm, Psalm 123, is a prayer uttered in the midst of hostility and the contempt of the world. Psalm 124 praises God for deliverance from enemies and declares that help comes from the Lord (v 8). The juxtaposition of these two psalms doesn't seem to be coincidental. The first five verses of Psalm 124 contain two 'if' clauses (vs 1,2) and three 'then' clauses (vs 3–5), which spell out that 'if' God had not been on their side, 'then' disaster would have happened to them.

The attack of the angry and destructive enemy is compared to a raging torrent that would engulf God's people (vs 2b–5). The 'flood', 'torrent' and 'raging waters' in the Old Testament often refer to the forces opposed to God and his faithful.[2] We can imagine that God's people are facing a horrendous threat from their enemies, even though the menace is not specifically identified here. The metaphor of a bird escaping from a trap (v 7) indicates that they have survived the crisis up to this point, which elicits communal praise to God and evokes faith in God's deliverance in future.

To affirm that God is 'on our side' (vs 1,2) and that 'our help' comes from the Lord (v 8) is to admit our incapability in securing our own life and future. Only by this fundamental recognition and humility shall we be driven to seek the ultimate source of power – 'the Maker of heaven and earth' (v 8).

'If God is for us, who can be against us?'[3] We shall not fear, as God is 'our refuge and strength, an ever-present help in trouble'.[4]

---

[1] Rom 8:32 [2] Eg Ps 46:1–3; 74:12–15; 89:8–10; 93:3,4 [3] Rom 8:31 [4] Ps 46:1

BIBLE IN A YEAR: **Exodus 21,22; Psalm 16**

Ultimate Source of Power

May I see no one except Jesus! O Lord, help me to fix my eyes on God solely, instead of on humans! Remove from me the things that are distracting!

The opening reports (vs 1–9;10–13) and closing reports (vs 22,23;24,25) on Jehoahaz and Jehoash (the second and third kings in the line of Jehu) resonate with the fortunes of Israel in its struggle against Aramaean domination. The death of Elisha lies in the central piece of the sandwiched structure (vs 14–21). Knowing that Elisha is fatally ill, Jehoash goes to visit the prophet. The king is devastated and frightened of facing the future without the presence and power of Elisha after his death (v 14). The prophet then offers Jehoash two signs for assurance. First, Elisha instructs the king to take a bow and arrows and shoot, which ensures Israel's victory over Aram (vs 15–17). Second, the prophet tells Jehoash to take the arrows and strike the ground with them. He does this, but he is rebuked for striking only three times instead of five or six times. This indicates that Jehoash will defeat Aram only three times (vs 18,19; see also vs 24,25).

Elisha had disappeared after Jehu's anointing as king in chapter 9. His resurfacing in chapter 13 comes with his imminent death, which prophetically indicates the end of Jehu's dynasty. Not only does the king's shooting and striking the ground with the arrows symbolise God's grace despite the impending judgement, but the prophet embodies it. After Elisha's death, a dead man is buried and his corpse is thrown into the prophet's grave hastily when a band of Moabites are seen to invade Israel. Miraculously the dead man is revived as his body touches Elisha's bones (vs 20,21). It recalls one last time the divine power in both life and death of the prophet. God's protection still continues despite Elisha's death.

Is our attention drawn to the powerful leaders instead of the source of their power? Give credit to God, who pours his grace through human leaders – even beyond their lifetime.

BIBLE IN A YEAR: **Exodus 23,24; Acts 26**

2 Kings 14

Unfathomable Sovereignty

Father! Open our eyes to see what you see. Lead us in the light of your truth. Grant us a fervent hunger and desire for your perspective evermore!

This chapter indicates that, instead of exclusive favour towards Judah, God also shows his special interest in Israel. Although Amaziah king of Judah attempts to do good (vs 3–6) and triumphs over Edom (v 7), Judah is defeated by Jehoash king of Israel (vs 12–14). Highlighting Israel's achievement, Jehoash's 'might' (v 15, NRSV)[1] is mentioned in contrast to Amaziah's 'deeds' (v 18, NRSV). Compared with Jehoash's peaceful death (v 16), Amaziah is murdered in a conspiracy against him (vs 19,20). The attention quickly shifts to Israel after a brief report of Amaziah's successor, Azariah (vs 21,22).

God's will to bless Jehu's house[2] is apparent in the reign of Jeroboam II, king of Israel (vs 23–29). Despite the negative evaluation of his reign (v 24) – like that of his father Jehoash[3] – Jeroboam II expands Israel's territory as far as Solomon's, according to the prophecy of Jonah (v 25) and he recovers Damascus and Hamath, which belonged to Judah. Again, as with his father, the 'might' of Jeroboam II is highlighted (v 28, NRSV). Seeing the distress of Israel, God delivers his people temporarily through Jeroboam II (vs 26,27). Throughout the chapter, God's sovereignty is repeatedly demonstrated by his special favour towards Israel despite its sinfulness.

Judging from a human perspective, some people may find God's way of dealing with Judah and Israel in this chapter unthinkable. As Paul reminds us, however, we receive God's blessing solely out of his grace, not by our deeds.[4] More importantly, God is the ultimate judge; the timing of judgement is in his hand: 'because I will soon punish the house of Jehu for the massacre at Jezreel'.[5]

O Lord, we are in awe of your inscrutable sovereignty. May our faith be anchored in your perfect justice and steadfast love, even when your will is beyond human comprehension.

[1] Cf 2 Kings 13:12 [2] 2 Kings 10:30 [3] Cf 2 Kings 13:11 [4] Rom 9:15,16 [5] Hos 1:4

BIBLE IN A YEAR: **Exodus 25,26; Acts 27**

Mind your Health

'The LORD is near to all who call on him, to all who call on him in truth. He fulfils the desires of those who fear him'.[1]

This chapter reports on the last kings of Israel – Zechariah, Shallum, Menahem, Pekahiah and Pekah. Fulfilling God's promise (v 12),[2] Jehu's dynasty lasts till the fourth generation – Zechariah, who is assassinated by Shallum (v 10). Though Shallum receives no assessment, his short reign (one month) conveys a negative evaluation in itself. The other four kings receive the same negative verdict of persistently doing evil according to the sins of Jeroboam son of Nebat (vs 9,18,24,28). The references to this evaluative formula outnumber those in other chapters of the book. Rapid succession, assassinations, coups, conspiracies and foreign interventions mark these final kings' regimes.

The record of five kings of Israel (vs 8–31) is sandwiched between the summary of two kings of Judah, Azariah (also called Uzziah; vs 1–7) and Jotham (vs 32–38).

These two southern kings are commended for doing what is right in God's eyes, except for failing to remove the high places (vs 3,4;34,35). This account does not explain Azariah's affliction with leprosy (v 5), whereas Chronicles views it as a divine discipline for his arrogance in offering incense in the Temple.[3] Though the reigns of Azariah and Jotham in Judah are relatively long and stable compared with those in Israel, Azariah's leprosy and the foreign invasion during Jotham's rule (v 37) suggest that Judah is not free of trouble.

Our sins pose far-reaching impact upon our offspring, just as Israel's first king affects the reigns and people after him. Eventually it costs the nation. Half-hearted commitment is equally offensive: Azariah and Jotham's failure to remove the high places displeases God, despite their attempts to do good in other respects.

Sin threatens not only our own lives but also those of people who come after us. To secure our spiritual health, we need regular health checks by the Holy Spirit.

---

[1] Ps 145:18,19 [2] See also 2 Kings 10:30 [3] 2 Chr 26:16–20

BIBLE IN A YEAR: **Exodus 27,28; Acts 28**

2 Kings 16

God's Standard Only

O blessed Lord, I come to find rest in your presence. Shape within me a heart after your own heart.

Ahaz, unlike David, does not do what is right in the eyes of God (v 2). He is condemned for walking in the ways of Israel's kings (v 3a). How? Like Israel, he follows the Canaanite practice by sacrificing his son in the fire (v 3b), which is counted as a reason for Israel's doom.[1] Like Israel, Ahaz worships at the high places (v 4).[2] The sins of Jeroboam son of Nebat are presented as the cause of Israel's downfall.[3] The unusual comparison of Ahaz with the kings of Israel reveals the author's deliberate technique of mirroring here. Facing the threat from Aram and Israel, Ahaz turns to Assyria for help (vs 5–9). Like Israel's foreign policies, those of Ahaz pave the way for the same fate of destruction.[4] The loss of Elath to Aram and then to Edom clearly indicates God's judgement on Judah (v 6).[5]

Meeting with his Assyrian suzerain in Damascus, Ahaz is impressed by a Syrian altar and he determines to build one on this model (vs 10,11). On his return to Jerusalem, Ahaz dedicates the new altar by making offerings (vs 12,13). He moves the old bronze altar (v 14) and uses it for seeking guidance (v 15). All these changes are implemented to please Assyria (v 18). To sum up, Ahaz lives by the standards of others instead of those of God.

Without following God's ways, Ahaz tries to keep his inheritance for his own well-being, but ironically he loses it. To curry favour with the Assyrian king, he loses God's favour. How often do we please humans more than God? Do we conform to the values of the world instead of doing the right things in God's eyes? May the following words be our prayer:

Dear Lord, by your grace help me live up to your standard so that your name may be glorified. I desire to serve you and live for you alone.

---

[1] 2 Kings 17:17,18 [2] Cf 2 Kings 17:9–11 [3] 2 Kings 14:24; 15:9,18,24,28 [4] 2 Kings 17:19,20 [5] Cf Deut 28:52,63

BIBLE IN A YEAR: **Exodus 29,30; Psalm 17**

God's Alarm Buzzer!

Abba Father, help me to know your voice and not be distracted by other voices. Increase my awareness and sensitivity to the Holy Spirit in discerning your will!

After recording the fall of Israel to Assyria (vs 1–6), this passage offers a theological commentary on the disaster (vs 7–23). Despite his evil deeds (v 2), Hoshea, the last king of Israel, is described as not being as bad as the preceding kings. He is not accorded the negative evaluation of the kings of Israel, comparing them to the sins of Jeroboam son of Nebat.[1] Such toning down of criticism contrasts with that of Ahaz king of Judah, who is blamed for following 'the ways of the kings of Israel'.[2]

The people are held accountable for Israel's destruction (vs 7–17), but the kings bear the major part of the blame (v 8). The section closes with the conclusion that the sinfulness of the Israelites is tied in with the kingship of Jeroboam son of Nebat, who led them to sin (vs 21–23). The wordplays in the passage elicit a strong sense of divine justice. The people of Israel 'rejected' God's law and covenant (v 15) so God 'rejected' them (v 20). The Israelites did not depart from their sins (v 22; TNIV 'turn away') so God caused them to depart (v 23; TNIV 'removed'). Israel's downfall serves as a warning to Judah, but unfortunately Judah 'followed the practices Israel had introduced' (v 19). The narrator foresees Judah's fate with Israel's exile in hindsight. It is no coincidence that the Hebrew wording in verse 23, 'So Israel went into exile from its land' parallels the later 'So Judah went into exile from its land'[3] (the parallel is obscured by TNIV).

God never executes judgement without ringing the alarm buzzer. He sends his servants to give warnings (v 13). He even uses someone's failure to alert us, just as he uses Israel's exile to warn Judah. The Holy Spirit within rebukes and admonishes us too.

When God's security alarm is buzzing, how do you respond? Obedient heart? Or deaf ears?

---

[1] Cf 1 Kings 16:2,19,26,31; 22:52; 2 Kings 3:3; 9:9; 10:29; 13:2,11; 14:24 [2] 2 Kings 16:3 [3] 2 Kings 25:21

BIBLE IN A YEAR: **Exodus 31,32; Matthew 1**

2 Kings 17:24–41

Illuminating our Blindness

'Open my eyes that I may see wonderful things in your law.'[1]

Our attention turns to the resettled Samaria. To destroy the cohesion of the Israelites remaining in Samaria, the Assyrians deport the Israelites to various parts of the Assyrian Empire, replacing them with captives from other lands (v 24). Since the newly imported foreigners do not worship the Lord, God sends lions against them to warn them of his anger (v 25). This indicates that, being subject to the same commandments, these outsiders in the land are invited into the covenant as well, revealing God's heart for Gentiles. In desiring to know how to worship and please the God of that land, these foreigners are more sensitive to God's warnings than his own people.

Ironically, a priest, who was exiled for his apostasy, now returns to Bethel to teach those who replace him how to worship the Lord (v 27). How can such a flawed guide lead them? Both will fall into a pit.[2] The sins of Jeroboam son of Nebat extend beyond the doom of Israel. These foreign peoples imitate the Israelites' worst syncretistic practice – worshipping both the Lord and other gods from many lands (vs 32,33,41). Such mixed worship violates the covenant grounded in the law (vs 35–38), as this jealous God demands exclusive loyalty from his people. Sadly, these foreigners' syncretistic custom continues for generations, to the time when this text was written (vs 34,41).

'God is spirit, and his worshippers must worship in the Spirit and in truth.'[3] We must worship as instructed in his Word. To avoid blind leadership, remaining sensitive to the instruction of the Spirit, church leaders must solidly ground their teaching in Scripture. Since we all are 'a chosen people, a royal priesthood, a holy nation',[4] over-reliance on our leaders to feed us is unhealthy. The Holy Spirit can enlighten each individual if we desire to know his truth.

Spirit of truth, come and guide me into all the truth.[5]

---

[1] Ps 119:18 [2] Matt 15:14 [3] John 4:24 [4] 1 Pet 2:9; cf Rev 1:6 [5] John 16:13

BIBLE IN A YEAR: **Exodus 33,34; Matthew 2**

Security Under Strain

The light of God guides me. / The love of God surrounds me. / The shield of God protects me. / The peace of God fills me.

The term 'sceptre' often occurs in the contexts of sovereignty.[1] 'The sceptre of the wicked' (v 3a) therefore refers to the rule of the wicked kings, who may be from the community of faith (eg Manasseh, Ahab, Ahaz) or outside the community of faith (Assyrian, Babylonian or Persian). God's people are under severe strain, as the wicked are in control of the allotted territory of the righteous. There are hints of a threatening possibility that the righteous might use their hands to do evil (v 3b). If the wicked continue to persecute God's people, God's people might cease to be loyal to the Lord.

Despite the challenging circumstances, the psalmist's utterance exudes a deep sense of trust. First, that those who trust the Lord are as secure as Mount Zion, which is the immovable, everlasting symbol of God's presence in the world (v 1). Second, just as Jerusalem is surrounded by mountains, those who trust the Lord are surrounded by God's protection for ever (v 2). Third, the rule of the wicked will not last for ever, as God will banish them from his people's land (vs 3a,5a). Fourth, the declaration of peace on Israel is uttered longingly (v 5b). Finally, the psalmist pleads to God to do good to those who are good and upright in heart (v 4). This petition reflects his confidence in God's execution of justice for his faithful servants.

Similarly, God's people today are certainly not living in a vacuum, free of evils, troubles and trials. There are times when we are under difficult circumstances that challenge our faith. There are pressing moments when we are tempted to turn our backs on God. Amid such crises, may we hold fast to our faith in a secure God, who protects and vindicates.

Father, when life feels like spinning out of control, remind me that you reign over the world and over my life's circumstances. Help me to find peace in you.

[1] Cf Ps 2:9 (NIV note); 45:6; Isa 14:5

BIBLE IN A YEAR: **Exodus 35,36; Psalm 18**

2 Kings 18

Faith-Shaking Trials

Father, help me to stay alert spiritually, so that evils won't catch me by surprise. Feed my spirit with your holy words, so that I may resist sinning against you.

Hezekiah, king of Judah, is forced to pay tribute to Assyria after Sennacherib's attack (vs 13–16). Later, three Assyrian messengers come to threaten Judah to surrender (vs 17–37) by making faith-shaking arguments as follows. In the first speech, the Assyrian spokesman argues that it is dangerous for Judah to rely on Egypt (v 21), and that it is futile for Judah to rely on her own military (vs 23,24). The speaker tells lies, saying that it is unwise to trust in God because Hezekiah king of Judah has angered the Lord (v 22). The Assyrians even claim to be God's agent to destroy Judah (v 25).

In the second speech, the Assyrian spokesman deliberately speaks in Judah's language instead of Aramaic (the international language) so the people sitting on the wall will understand the message (vs 26,28). This propaganda aims to shake people's confidence in their king. Four times he denounces Judah's king (vs 29,30,31,32). Apart from comparing Hezekiah's empty promises to the benevolence of the Assyrian king (vs 31,32), the Assyrian speaker compares the Lord unfavourably to Assyrian gods and the gods of other nawtions already conquered (vs 33–35). The failure of any gods to deliver Samaria is clear evidence (v 34; cf vs 9–12). Can Hezekiah hold fast to the Lord and resist the Assyrian threat, but still survive?

If you were Hezekiah, how would you respond? The devil sometimes haunts us by undermining our dignity, other people's confidence in us and even our faith in God. May the Holy Spirit help us in discerning Satan's cunning lies and twisted arguments.

'Blessed are those who persevere under trial, because when they have stood the test, they will receive the crown of life that God has promised to those who love him.'[1]

---

[1] James 1:12, TNIV

BIBLE IN A YEAR: **Exodus 37,38; Matthew 3**

Faith-Growing Trials

Heavenly Father, your gift of Jesus as our Saviour gives us every reason to trust you completely.

Three rounds of threats posed by Sennacherib are recorded in chapters 18 and 19. First, Sennacherib comes to attack Judah and forces Hezekiah to pay tribute (18:13,14). In response, Hezekiah gives in completely (18:15,16). In the second threat, Sennacherib sends his messengers with an army to threaten Judah to surrender (18:17–37). In today's chapter, Hezekiah responds to the crisis by turning to God and seeking counsel from Isaiah (vs 1–7). In the final round, Sennacherib sends a hostile letter to Hezekiah (vs 9–13). In this exchange, Hezekiah responds to Sennacherib's written threat by turning to God directly. Instead of asking Isaiah to pray for the people, he utters a lengthy prayer expressing his complete trust in God (vs 15–19).

Throughout these three crises, Hezekiah's faith in God is growing progressively as the enemy's hostility rockets. It is noteworthy that God's intervention on Hezekiah's behalf over the Assyrian threats intensifies accordingly. God seems to remain silent in the first crisis, which encourages Sennacherib to boast of himself and despise the God of Judah (cf 18:30; 19:10). Responding to the second threat through Isaiah, God promises to make Sennacherib return to Assyria, where he will be killed (19:6,7). In reaction to the third threat, God promises to deliver Jerusalem. Eventually, God ends the whole crisis by killing 185,000 of the Assyrian army and having Sennacherib assassinated.

To sum up, the divine intervention on Judah's behalf corresponds positively with Hezekiah's growing trust in the Lord, which eventually brings an end to the continual threats from Sennacherib.

'... without faith it is impossible to please God'.[1] When we step out in faith, we are stepping into God's promises, with a golden opportunity to encounter him vividly.

---

[1] Heb 11:6

BIBLE IN A YEAR: **Exodus 39,40; Matthew 4**

2 Kings 20

Complacency is Costly

'Blessed are the pure in heart, for they will see God.'[1] 'Surely God is good to Israel, to those who are pure in heart.'[2]

Despite the earlier good comments on Hezekiah,[3] the author does not shy away from disclosing the king's darker side. To reverse his fatal sickness, Hezekiah begs God to extend his life (vs 2,3). In response, God enables him to live 15 extra years and deliver Jerusalem from Assyria (vs 5,6). However, to safeguard the divine assurance, Hezekiah asks God for a sign (turning the shadow backwards for ten steps), a request that indicates his lack of faith (vs 8–11). Then, Hezekiah shows off the complete treasure of the nation for the covetous Babylonians (v 13). Isaiah warns that the king's pride and complacency will lead to the downfall of Judah, the plunder of the national treasures and the deportation of his descendants to Babylon (vs 14–18).

Hezekiah witnesses the fall of Israel caused by her apostasy. However, he does not take the judgement on Judah seriously. The king's self-centredness, short-sightedness, stupidity and complacency are further revealed in his response to Isaiah's rebuke and warning (v 19): '"The word of the LORD you have spoken is good," Hezekiah replied. For he thought, "Will there not be peace and security in my lifetime?"' Unfortunately, Hezekiah does nothing to ask God to stop the judgement from happening after his lifetime. He begs for a longer life, but he does not repent of his foolishness to whet the Babylonians' invasion appetite. He cares about his own well-being more than the national security of his descendants in the future.

When people become complacent in their faith, they disregard their mistakes and become self-focused without caring about the fate of others. Despite his praiseworthy achievements, Hezekiah's carefree complacency has eventually cost the nation.

Father, infuse me with a sense of urgency to follow your lead. Prompt me to take sin seriously. Help me to live a life that places you at the centre.

---

[1] Matt 5:8 [2] Ps 73:1 [3] 2 Kings 18:5

BIBLE IN A YEAR: **Leviticus 1–3; Matthew 5**

God-Centred Prayers

'Father, if you are willing, take this cup from me; yet not my will, but yours be done.'[1]

Manasseh's 55-year reign (v 1) is longer than that of any of the other kings of Judah. He is the only one whose misdeeds are written in the concluding formula (v 17), which is probably intended to highlight Manasseh as the worst king in Judah ever. There is no lack of evidence for this verdict. Manasseh undoes the religious reform of his father Hezekiah (v 3a). Instead of following the example of David and Solomon and the Law of Moses (vs 7,8), he adopts the Canaanites' abominable practices and his sin is even worse than those of the nations driven out by Israel (vs 2,9,11). Manasseh sacrifices his own son in the fire (v 6), as Ahaz did,[2] and he consults mediums and spiritualists (v 6) just like Saul.[3] He is compared unfavourably with Ahab king of Israel, who promoted Baal worship (v 3).[4] God will judge Judah according to the same plumb line used against Samaria and Ahab (v 13). Manasseh leads the people of Judah into sins (v 9) and the worship of idols (v 11). The evil deeds of the king and his people provoke God's anger (vs 6,15). Manasseh sheds innocent blood, causing the nation to commit social crimes (v 16). All in all, the damages caused by his long, corrupt leadership have made Judah's downfall inevitable.

With hindsight, the negative side of Hezekiah's prayer for sparing his life from a fatal illness is revealed. His son Manasseh starts his reign at the age of 12 (v 1). If the chronology is correct, Manasseh was born during Hezekiah's extra years. However, Manasseh's leadership makes Judah's downfall irreversible.[5] This is in addition to Hezekiah's error in showing off national treasures to the Babylonian envoys after his recovery.[6] His healing doesn't make him a humble king. Instead, national security is jeopardised by his pride.

An important point about prayer comes to mind – asking God that we might do his will instead of ours, even when obeying him seems to be difficult.

---

[1] Luke 22:42 [2] 2 Kings 16:3 [3] 1 Sam 28 [4] 1 Kings 16:29–33 [5] 2 Kings 23:26; 24:2,3 [6] 2 Kings 20:12,13

BIBLE IN A YEAR: **Leviticus 4,5; Psalm 19**

True Love of God

Gracious Father, we commit to loving you with all our hearts, souls and minds. In the same spirit, we commit to loving our neighbours as ourselves!

Two events about Josiah, king of Judah, are recorded in this chapter. First, he commands his officials to pay out the money that is in the Temple of God and to entrust it to the workers and supervisors there. Josiah makes sure that the funding for the Temple project goes to the workers and supervisors without exploitation (vs 3–7). Second, when Josiah hears the words of the Book of the Law, his reaction is impressive. He tears his robes and weeps before the Lord (vs 11,19). He sends the high priest and two officials to inquire of the Lord for himself, for the people and for all Judah about the judgement written in the book (v 13). Huldah the prophet points out that God will let Josiah die in peace because of the king's humility and responsive heart (vs 19,20).

We can quickly conclude from these two events that Josiah loves God, because he cares about the Temple of the Lord and he responds humbly to the words of the Lord. Some details about Josiah are noteworthy. Impressively, this king knows that the Temple workers and supervisors are honest people, to whom the money can be entrusted. This demonstrates that he is a down-to-earth king, caring about his people. His fervent endeavour to inquire of the Lord about the Book of the Law focuses not only on his own well-being but also on that of his people and the nation. One common point stands out in these events: Josiah's love of God is reflected in his love for the people.

The Pharisees in Jesus' time were actively involved in all sorts of religious activities that only reveal their interest in themselves instead of God and other people. True worship is never divorced from loving our neighbours.

May the Lord grant us Josiah's responsive heart and humility, rightly to love ourselves, God and other people.

BIBLE IN A YEAR: **Leviticus 6,7; Matthew 6**

Genuine Faith

'If Christianity is untrue, no honest man will want to believe it, however helpful it might be.'[1]

Josiah follows the Lord with all his heart, with all his soul and with all his strength (vs 3,25). His great effort to inquire of the Book of the Law,[2] renew the covenant with the Lord (vs 1–3), bring reforms to Judah (vs 4–20) and celebrate Passover across the nation (vs 21–24) has made him the best king ever in Israel's history: 'Neither before nor after Josiah was there a king like him who turned to the LORD as he did' (v 25). Then the text offers, side by side, the impending death of the nation (vs 26,27) and the tragic death of the king (vs 29,30). Josiah's good deeds cannot offset the destructive impact caused by Manasseh's sins. This righteous king dies young in a tragedy. His unsurpassable commitment to God cannot earn him a longer life, nor can it avert the destiny of Judah as prophesied by Huldah.[3] Poignantly, Josiah's untimely death symbolises the imminent destruction of the nation.

Even though Josiah knows that Judah's fate cannot be avoided, he still sets his mind to carry out religious reforms and lead the nation to follow God, which is utterly impressive. He makes every effort to keep God's commandments and maintain his faith, although he sees no hope of earning salvation by good deeds. All in all, the divine sovereignty stands out powerfully in the text. Commercial and religious transaction has no room to play in genuine faith and covenantal relationship with the Lord.

This reflection reminds me of the danger of a 'prosperity gospel' that only emphasises blessings from God – wealth, health, success, happiness, eternal life and so on. If this is our only motive for following Jesus, our faith will easily be swept away by adversity. We are not promised a smooth ride.

Jesus encourages his disciples to take the small gate and the narrow road that lead to life.[4] Jesus himself died for the sinful world, despite his complete blamelessness.

[1] CS Lewis, *God in the Dock*, Eerdmans, 2014, p109 [2] 2 Kings 22:12–20 [3] 2 Kings 22:16,17 [4] Matt 7:13,14

BIBLE IN A YEAR: **Leviticus 8,9; Matthew 7**

Psalm 126

Memory and Hope

'When upon life's billows you are tempest tossed, / when you are discouraged, thinking all is lost, / count your many blessings, name them one by one'.[1]

The repeated use of the verb 'restore' (vs 1,4) helps to define this psalm. The first use is in the past tense. The community remembers what the Lord did for his people in the past. The reference to restoring the fortunes of Zion (v 1) probably refers to the return of the Jewish exiles from Babylon. This dream-like experience brought great joy to God's people (vs 2,3) and it even surprised the surrounding nations (v 2) in those days.

The memory of God's restoration in the past (vs 1–3) becomes the rationale for the people's petition for God's restoration in the future (vs 4–6). Seeing God's faithfulness in the past helps us to find hope in the difficulties lying ahead. Counting our blessings requires a shift in perspective. Without seeing God, the wadi remains a dry river bed in the barren wilderness of the Negev. With God in sight, we anticipate a flowing stream in the Negev, bringing life to the desert (v 4b). Without seeing God, we may focus on our sorrow during the hardship ('tears', v 5a; 'weeping', v 6a). With God, we look forward to the joyful ending after perseverance (vs 5b,6b). It's a long wait between sowing and harvesting, but the hope built upon the previous bountiful harvest gives farmers patience and encouragement to endure the hardship until the harvest.

As Henri Nouwen puts it, 'By inviting God into our difficulties we ground life – even in its sad moments – in joy and hope.'[2] Thus weeping does not have the final say. No wonder the theme of joy permeates this psalm.

As we count our blessings, may the songs of joy keep sounding in our minds amid all the challenging times.

[1] Johnson Oatman, 1856–1922, 'Count your blessings' [2] Henri Nouwen, *Turn My Mourning into Dancing*, Nelson, 2001, pxv

BIBLE IN A YEAR: **Leviticus 10–12; Psalm 20**

2 Kings 23:36 – 24:20a

Seek his Divine Presence

**'My heart says of you, "Seek his face!" Your face, LORD, I will seek.'[1]
Lord, I long to embrace your presence, with peace in heart and soul.**

This passage records the lives of the last three kings of Judah – Jehoiakim, Jehoiachin and Zedekiah. The narrator of Kings unambiguously spells out the real cause of Judah's fall and exile to Babylon. It is not Nebuchadnezzar but God who sends this superpower to punish Judah (24:2), according to the prophetic word (v 13).[2] There are some common points about these three kings. First, each of their reigns is relatively short – eleven years each for Jehoiakim and Zedekiah, three months for Jehoiachin – marking the imminent death of the nation. Second, all three kings are blamed for doing evil in the eyes of the Lord (23:37; 24:9,19). Third, out of anger, God removes them from his presence (Jehoiakim, v 3; Zedekiah, v 20). The text specifically highlights that God thrusts Jehoiachin from his divine

presence by deporting him to Babylon along with the royal family, officials, fighting men and elites of the land (vs 14–16). The exile of Zedekiah and the fall of Judah to Babylon will be detailed in the next chapter.

Except for the narrator's report, we don't hear God's voice in these final accounts, as the Lord withdraws himself from his people.[3] A terrible silence of God can be felt everywhere throughout the text. Sin drives us away from the presence of God. Though he is omnipresent, our experience of his presence doesn't always match up. Learning from the negative examples of these last kings of Judah, may we strive to do what is right in the eyes of the Lord, not allowing sin to keep us away from his presence.

'Do not hide your face from me, do not turn your servant away in anger; you have been my helper. Do not reject me or forsake me, God my Saviour.'[4]

[1] Ps 27:8 [2] Cf 2 Kings 20:17; 21:10–15 [3] 2 Kings 24,25 [4] Ps 27:9

BIBLE IN A YEAR: **Leviticus 13,14; Matthew 8**

2 Kings 24:20b – 25:30

A Gleam of Hope

Father, I come here before you with a troubled heart. Help me to focus on your Word so that I can find hope in your unfailing love.

Zedekiah was the last king of Judah. His name means 'Justice of the Lord' in Hebrew, which ironically expresses God's justice in the closing chapter of the book. Judah falls under God's unrelenting judgement against her wilful disobedience.[1] Before the curtain falls, the camera pans to the exile in Babylon (vs 27–30). Because of the amnesty of Awel-Marduk king of Babylon, Jehoiachin king of Judah is released after 37 years of imprisonment and dines regularly at the Babylonian king's table. What does this epilogue mean to the Jewish exiles, whose hope is shattered by the destruction of the Temple (vs 13–17), the fall of Jerusalem (vs 8–10) and the humiliation of their last king Zedekiah (vs 1–7)? The release of Jehoiachin demonstrates God's unfailing promise to David – a survivor is preserved in the Davidic line.[2]

Despite the depressing accounts of Judah's downfall, the second book of Kings actually ends on a positive note – and this is not the final word. God's acts are yet to come as history unfolds. His divine promise to David is further realised when Zerubbabel (Jehoiachin's grandson) is appointed as the governor of the province of Judah by the Persians.[3] During the post-exilic period, Zerubbabel and Joshua the high priest co-lead the Jewish returnees in rebuilding the Temple in Jerusalem.[4] Although he is never a king on earth, a descendant of Jehoiachin and Zerubbabel would be born to play the role of a perfect righteous king.[5] This Messiah would deliver his people from darkness and forgive their sins.[6]

During dark times, it can be difficult to look beyond the negativity. May Jehoiachin's uplifting story rekindle our hope in God, who is greater than all highs and lows.

---

[1] 2 Kings 24,25 [2] 2 Sam 7:16; 2 Kings 8:19 [3] Hag 1:1 [4] Hag 2 [5] Matt 1:12–16; 2:2,6; 21:6–9; 27:11,29,37,42 [6] Col 1:13,14

BIBLE IN A YEAR: **Leviticus 15,16; Matthew 9**

Scripture Union
holidays
Fun-packed, faith-filled Christian holidays for 8- to 18-year-olds

BOOK ONLINE:
su.org.uk/holidays

count me in

WHAT ARE YOU DOING THIS SUMMER?

We're looking for volunteers to join our holiday teams. So, if you want to have the time of your life while helping children grow closer to Jesus, sign up today:
su.org.uk/countmein

David Smith

APOCALYPSE THEN AND NOW

There are certain words which seem, like hedgehogs, to lie dormant for a while. Then they suddenly appear and enter conversations, news bulletins and literature until, as the result of overuse, they start to sound like jargon and return to relative obscurity. Take the word 'icon'. Originally having a very specific meaning with deep religious significance, it was removed from this context to become a catch-all term applied promiscuously to buildings, events – even pop stars. Now, exhausted by so much exposure, it has receded to the margins of everyday language.

The word 'apocalyptic' has played a similar role in modern public discourse. Originally an obscure, technical term, it was propelled into the limelight by the war movie *Apocalypse Now*. The disturbing content of the film and the tragic historical events it purported to depict effectively defined the meaning of the word in public consciousness and suddenly it began to be used with regard to all kinds of disasters and catastrophes. The infamous attack on the Twin Towers in New York, the subsequent war on terror and the invasion of Iraq resulted in many Christians in the United States, including at least one American President, linking such events with the visions found in the final book in the Bible, John's 'Apocalypse'.

The word itself is a translation of the Greek term *apokalypsis*, meaning 'revelation'. It was applied to a particular style of writing which began to appear among the Jewish people in Palestine during the second century before Christ. This was a period of great suffering when – neither for the first nor the last time – the Jews faced a reign of terror which threatened them with extinction. This is the context of the book of Daniel, which clearly reflects the terrible danger he and his companions faced and contains apocalyptic visions by means of which people of faith were able to transcend their historical context and view their situation from the perspective of the throne of God. Apocalyptic is thus a language of crisis. Like an underground stream, it 'has flowed on undetected, sometimes for centuries at a time, breaking surface every now and again, particularly in times of crisis and persecution, to bring refreshment and strength to the harassed people of God.'[1]

---

[1] DS Russell, *Apocalyptic: Ancient and Modern*, Fortress Press, 1968, p6

The threat to the faith of Israel in Daniel's time came from the spread and dominance of Hellenistic (Greek) culture, which, while brilliant in many respects, demanded an absolute submission to a ruler, Antiochus, who, in 169 BC, assumed the title 'Epiphanes' – God manifest! For the Jewish people, who had endeavoured to serve the state and had won respect for their wisdom and faithfulness, the claim that political rulers were divine and must not only be obeyed but worshipped, amounted to blasphemy and demanded resistance. This is a theme that runs through the entire Bible, from Abraham in quest of the 'city with foundations'[2] to John of Patmos as a lonely exile 'because of the word of God and the testimony of Jesus'.[3] In precisely such contexts, prophetic revelation has taken the form of apocalyptic visions by which faith in the Lord is strengthened in a time of great suffering and hope is renewed that the ultimate triumph belongs to Israel's God and his Messiah.

If Daniel's context was one in which faith in God demanded a costly and countercultural obedience, this was even more true in the world of Jesus and his apostles. The first-century Jewish historian Josephus wrote an account of the conflict between Jews and Romans throughout the first century, in which he depicts 'carnage, piracy, massacres, and the wholesale crucifixion and burning of insurgents'. It has been said that we will not understand the social and cultural context of Jesus and the early church 'without coming to grips with such terror and suffering' and that to ignore this must result in 'a grievous misunderstanding of the world in which Jews and the Jewish Christians of the period were living'.[4]

It is precisely this context which explains the appearance of apocalyptic literature in the New Testament, both in the Gospels[5] and, of course, in the book of Revelation. There are obviously great challenges with regard to the contemporary interpretation of literature of this kind, and throughout Christian history there have been examples of bizarre readings of these texts. We are limited here to suggesting a few guiding principles in the understanding of the apocalyptic passages in the Bible.

First, in contexts of great suffering, or times when evil seems to be triumphant, the authors of such visions are inspired by the Holy Spirit to imagine a different,

[2] Heb 11:10 [3] Rev 1:9 [4] Richard Fenn, *The Death of Herod: An Essay in the Sociology of Religion*, Cambridge University Press, 1992, p171 [5] Eg Mark 13

transformed world. These writers and their hearers were probably facing surveillance and risked retribution should their work appear to be seditious. Thus the language they employed and the array of symbols, including systems of numbering, will have functioned as a kind of code, understood by those for whom it was intended but mystifying to state authorities (and sometimes to us!). The word *imagine* is crucially important here, since apocalyptic literature involves great creativity and the faith to envisage a different kind of world in times when the powers-that-be seek to impose their way as the only one available. Richard Bauckham, in the best introduction to the book of Revelation known to me, writes that it 'tackles peoples' imaginative response to the world, which is at least as deep and influential as their intellectual convictions.'[6]

Second, apocalyptic authors call for radical, costly discipleship and seek to resist any compromise between God and mammon. The context for the visions of John of Patmos is not only the dominant – and apparently triumphant – Roman Empire but also the tragedy of the failure of so many of the congregations he knows

and loves to stand firm in their confession of the lordship of the crucified Jesus. Most of the churches of Asia Minor described in chapters 2 and 3 are involved in some form of compromise, seen most clearly in the Laodicean delusion that its material wealth signified success, when the reality was that this facing-both-ways church was 'wretched, pitiful, poor, blind and naked'.[7] There is nothing that is obscure in this message, except that the vision of Christians who possess great wealth in an unjust world may be so distorted that they are incapable of accepting the reality of their hypocrisy.

Third, the thrust of the book as a whole is to encourage patience and faithfulness in the light of the transcendent reality which is revealed to those who pass through the 'door standing open in heaven'[8] and so enter the throne room of God. That door, together with the summons to 'Come up here',[9] is the turning point of the book, since it enables John – and us with him – to leave behind the empirical reality of a world in which no escape seems possible from the imperial power of Rome and to gain a perspective from heaven in which everything is changed! Rome is now seen as a beast, ruling on

---

[6] Richard Bauckham, *The Theology of the Book of Revelation*, Cambridge University Press, 1993, p159
[7] Rev 3:17 [8] Rev 4:1 [9] Rev 4:1

the basis of military might but devoid of moral power. History has not been closed with the end of *pax Romana*: it remains open to the redemptive power of the slain Lamb who is alone *worthy* to open the scroll with seven seals. This does not mean that the suffering of the faithful is over, or that the reality of pain and death is now suppressed and only praise and celebration are valid. Even the saints in heaven still cry out in the language of the psalms of lament: 'How long, Sovereign Lord ...?',[10] and are told to wait a little longer until the fruits of redemption are complete and peoples of the world will discover the tree of life whose leaves are 'for the healing of the nations'.[11]

Fourth, the vision of John of Patmos presents a challenge to the urban empire of Rome and, by implication, to the endless city of the urban world of today, with its stunning depiction of the New Jerusalem. Justo Gonzalez writes that Rome considered itself to be the great civiliser on account of the magnificence of the city of Rome itself and because the Romans had built cities everywhere throughout the empire on the same urban model. Yet in Revelation 18, perhaps the most terrifying text in the Bible, the glory that was Rome is exposed as being built upon what would today be called global injustice and is declared to be unsustainable since it will collapse under the holy judgement of the righteous God. By contrast, the holy city, New Jerusalem, comes down from heaven and, most mind-blowing of all, God himself takes up residence within it as 'the old order of things has passed away'.[12] We move here beyond what our feeble intelligence is capable of grasping, but such is the nature of apocalyptic writing that it offers us a hope which is both real and yet beyond our wildest imagination.

FOR FURTHER READING

There has been a surge of scholarly interest in apocalyptic literature in general and Revelation in particular. Of the two books that I particularly recommend, that by Keller is the more demanding:

Justo Gonzalez, *For The Healing of the Nations: The Book of Revelation in an Age of Cultural Conflict*, Orbis Books, 1999
Catherine Keller, *Facing Apocalypse: Climate, Democracy, and Other Last Chances*, Orbis Books, 2021

---

[10] Rev 6:10 [11] Rev 22:2 [12] Rev 21:4

Ephesians

GOD'S COSMIC PLAN OF BLESSING

Ephesians reveals to us the wonderful mystery of God's work, to draw all people to Christ and, in Christ, to create a new humanity. This new humanity is blessed by God and reconciled to him. It will extend that reconciliation and blessing to others and, in doing so, it will enable the powers that stand against God to be exposed.

Ephesus was a large city in the first century, with a minority Jewish population and four impressive temples to pagan gods, including the enormous temple to Artemis. It was a city of competing religions, where Paul had planted a church and then returned to minister there for over two years.[1] Paul is writing to encourage the believers to stand firm in their faith in Christ. He begins his letter by describing the revolutionary reality that Christ has brought into existence, before instructing the Ephesian believers on how they are to live to display this new reality to one another and the world around them.

Paul is writing from prison, a hugely challenging environment: uncomfortable, with little food or light, alongside other prisoners who were most likely sick and nearing death. Given this, it is even more remarkable how Paul's words are filled with hope and life.

There is scholarly debate about the authorship of Ephesians, but these notes accept the statement in 1:1 that the author is Paul, an apostle of Christ Jesus. The letter contains sections of complex theology (4:7–10) and contentious theology (5:21–33; 6:5–9). There is further reading below to help readers to explore these areas more fully.

David Horsfall

FOR FURTHER READING

On authorship: David DeSilva, *An Introduction to the New Testament,* Apollos, 2004, p716–721
For a classic devotional approach: John Stott, *The Message of Ephesians,* IVP, 1991
For a contemporary technical but pastoral commentary: Lynn Cohick, *The Letter to the Ephesians,* Eerdmans, 2020
For a complementary approach: Andrew Lincoln, *Ephesians,* Thomas Nelson, 1990

---

[1] Acts 18–20

Are You Blessed?

Generous Father, I praise you for lavishing grace upon me. Lord Jesus, I praise you for redeeming me. Holy Spirit, I praise you for marking me as God's own.

Who do you think the blessed people in the world are? If you lived in Paul's day, there were two groups often considered blessed. The Greeks thought that those free from the fragilities of life were blessed: those who did not need to toil. This usually meant the rich, who were free from cares, or the dead, who were free from grief. Jewish people thought those who had God as their Lord, who trusted in him and obeyed him, were blessed. Their signs of being blessed were long life, prosperity, honour and security in God.

Paul, however, writes that the blessed person is one who has been blessed by God with every spiritual blessing in Christ. In one long sentence (in the Greek), he moves between praising God, extolling him for his multifaceted work on our behalf and describing his character.

In love, God has acted for you, with all wisdom and understanding, according to the wealth of his grace and in accordance with his plan and pleasure. God is pleased to bless you.

The blessing God gives is not to be transported away from life's tough times, nor to be guaranteed wealth, children or long life. It is to be chosen, holy and blameless, adopted, redeemed, forgiven, included and marked as someone who will receive a glorious inheritance. What do we look at when we consider whether we are blessed? To our bank account, our children or grandchildren, our careers, or our reputation with others? Paul reminds us to look at God and consider what he has done for us, for then we find that we are blessed beyond measure with blessings that will not spoil or fade.

Go through Paul's list and note down which blessings you need God to reconfirm in your heart and mind today.

BIBLE IN A YEAR: **Leviticus 17,18; Matthew 10**

Ephesians 1:15–23

Rightly Thankful?

Jesus, you are the Way, the Truth and the Life; draw my heart to dwell on that. Cause thankfulness to rise in me because I can trust you.

Thanksgiving is always the second word, never the first.[1] When we are thankful, it is a response to something that has happened to us. Our thanksgiving often arises out of pleasant and prosperous external circumstances. Your life takes a turn for the better and the natural response is to be pleased; we can turn this into thanksgiving, that our Father has given us a good gift.

Paul is thankful, not because this life is going well for him but because God is actively at work in himself and others. Paul has been beaten, imprisoned, rejected and shipwrecked, and yet he chooses to be overflowing with thanksgiving, something he also instructs the church to be.[2] How can he respond like this? His eyes are fixed on what truly matters, trusting in the Lord Jesus and loving others. When he does so, he gives thanks. Paul uses hyperbole to show how thankful he is that the Ephesians have faith and that they show love: he says he never stops giving thanks.

It is from this place that his prayer for the church is born. He prays that the church will grow, not in material ways (though these can be blessings), but in wisdom and revelation so that we may know God better. He prays that we may be enlightened to know the hope of a glorious inheritance and the power of God to raise us from the dead. As God has placed Christ as head over all things and disarmed the powers who stand against him, our hope is secured. Therefore, we always have a reason to give thanks, even in the darkest moments. This is our buttress against the temptation to despair. Thanksgiving is always the second word, never the first.

Set aside ten minutes to focus on giving thanks to God, not for circumstances but simply for the gift of Jesus and the Spirit.

---

[1] PT O'Brien, 'Thanksgiving', in *Dictionary of Paul and his Letters*, ed Gerald F Hawthorne and Ralph P Martin, IVP, 1993, p696 [2] 1 Thess 5:18

BIBLE IN A YEAR: **Leviticus 19,20; Psalm 21**

Ephesians 2:1–10

The Heart of the Story

Father, you have taken me from a pit to your throne and from death to life in Christ. This is your gift to me, and I give you my adoration.

Have you ever tried to sum up the story of Scripture in 60 seconds? If Paul had to, I wonder if these ten verses would be what he would say. At the heart of the story is the great love and rich mercy of God. A love and mercy that transform death into life and disobedient wanderings into being seated on the very throne of God with Christ. These verses take us to the heart of both God's character and his action.

There are times in life when we need gentle guidance to head in the right direction. Maybe it is a parent holding onto our saddle as we learn to ride a bike or a grandmother guiding our hand as we add ingredients to a dinner. We learn from practice and gradually improve and become independent. The story of Scripture is not that kind of story. It is a story of God's powerful resurrection that creates life out of death. A story of God's merciful honouring of those who dismissed the king, treating them with such kindness they end up seated on his throne. It is a story of grace, the unmerited gift of God that both humbles and exalts us.

Tim Keller wrote of the gospel: 'We are so evil and sinful and flawed that Jesus had to die for us ... But we are so loved and valued that he was willing to die for us'.[1] These verses reveal our plight, and it is bleak. Yet even as the darkness draws around us, the light of the love and mercy of God breaks through and banishes even the faintest glimpse of a shadow. That is a story that has the power to change the whole of creation.

Write out your testimony of coming to faith in God and use it to worship God as you see your place in his amazing story.

---

[1] Tim Keller, *The Meaning of Marriage*, Hodder & Stoughton, 2011, p166

BIBLE IN A YEAR: **Leviticus 21,22; Matthew 11**

Who, them?

Jesus Christ, by your blood the whole of humanity is brought near; in your flesh, a new humanity is created. Mould my heart to live in this truth.

A Jewish person in Jerusalem would have lived in the shadow of the Temple. This site was connected to the belief that God had once dwelt alongside his people in the land and the hope that he would return and do so again. The Temple displayed the hope of the intimate closeness of God, but also the separation between God and humanity due to sin. A Gentile would have been viewed as someone excluded both from the people of God and from the blessing of God. It has long been a human trait to create groups of people who are included and others who are excluded.

God's work in Jesus Christ rends the very fabric of reality and creates a new order. Those who were far off now have peace with God: they are brought near. Maybe more challenging is when Paul writes that the barrier, the dividing wall of hostility, has been destroyed. Those markers which were used to separate people have now been dismantled and the two groups are recreated, as one new people. Throughout the passage, Paul repeats the word peace: Jesus is our peace, the new humanity is at peace, and Jesus preached peace. Peace, here, does not mean tranquillity, but the daily sacrificial work of reconciliation and unity that the church is to embody.

Paul's call to the Jew and the Gentile was to see that now they are one group, fellow citizens and members of the same house. They have been united by Jesus. That long-awaited hope that God would return to dwell with his people was happening, not in the physical Temple but rather in the beauty of the diverse church. We are called to cross barriers, extend apologies, break down walls and see others as our family, not our enemy.

If there is a broken relationship in your life, what does it look like to extend peace? Spend time praying for the person and asking the Spirit for healing.

BIBLE IN A YEAR: **Leviticus 23; Matthew 12; Psalm 22**

Whose House? God's House

Father, remind me that as you rested on the seventh day so I too should rest. Remind me that I am to work, but you are the only Lord.

This psalm is attributed to Solomon, the king who built the Temple of the Lord.[1] The Temple would be the central place for the people of God, even the centre point of the universe, as the meeting point between heaven and earth. If anyone could be forgiven for thinking that the building was the main focus, it would be Solomon. He poured so much time, people and resources into the physical structure of the Temple: it would have been an awe-inspiring sight in its day. Solomon displays in this psalm, however, that at the end of the day, without the presence and activity of God, it is just a building.

There is of course a balance to strike between working hard and overworking, between trusting God and passivity. The psalmist reminds us that even if we work hard, we are to remember that if our work prospers, it is a gift from the Lord: if it does not prosper, we still have the Lord as our inheritance. In the same way, we can work hard to invest in the lives of the children around us, but we need to remember that if there is spiritual fruit, it is the gift of God. If we cannot perceive any spiritual fruit, the children are still his gift to us.

Without this perspective, the result of our work becomes a source of pride for us or will be the main factor deciding our well-being. Without this perspective, we will be fearful about the future of our children. When we see work and children as gifts from the Lord and we trust that he is at work and will ultimately bring about his purposes, we can rest and enjoy his gifts.

Spend time giving the work of your hands and the children in your lives to the Lord. Ask him to release you from pride and fear. Enjoy and rest.

[1] 1 Kings 6

BIBLE IN A YEAR: **Leviticus 24,25; Psalm 23**

Who, me?

Jesus, you have made us your ambassadors. Let your grace be powerfully at work in us to shape us into messengers ready to share the riches of your love.

Have you ever thought you were heading on the right path and doing the right things, only for God to reveal a whole new direction? Paul was a Pharisee, who sought to keep the entire Law of God, so he knew how the Gentiles fell short. To this zealous man, Jesus revealed a mystery, that the people Paul thought were excluded would share the same promises God had given to Israel. More than this, Paul himself would be the one to proclaim the boundless riches of Christ to them.

Following God requires humility, because we must accept that there are times when we do not see where the path leads or what the whole plan is. I wonder if God sometimes keeps these things intentionally hidden from us so that we must make the choice to trust him, rather than ploughing ahead alone. Paul was committed to his life as a Pharisee[1] and he was good at it.[2] He was a man of conviction and ability. When Christ revealed himself to him on the Damascus Road, he had a choice. Would he humble himself before God, or reject him and continue on his way? When faced with the reality of God's plans, what do you do?

God reveals his plan: those who we might think are excluded should not to be considered far from Jesus. God's good news is for all people, the people we love and cherish, those who hate you and curse you, and those who are different to you. As the church, we display this divine wisdom to earth and heaven when we humbly walk in faith that we too can be messengers to people we never dreamed of. It is God's grace, not our skill, that fuels us.

Who comes to mind as someone you think is far from Jesus? Spend time praying for them and ask God how you might bless them today.

[1] Phil 3:4–6 [2] Gal 1:14

BIBLE IN A YEAR: **Leviticus 26,27; Matthew 13**

Ephesians 3:14–21

What Should I Pray For?

Father, I often give you my cares and my needs. Today I ask you to fill me with the knowledge of the depth of love Christ Jesus has for me.

Paul knew about hardships and worries and so did the churches he planted. As already noted, Paul suffered beatings, stoning, slander and arrest for preaching the gospel. The churches he was in relationship with experienced the difficulties of infighting, false accusations from opponents, poverty, sexual failings and factions developing. This makes Paul's prayer life, documented in the Scriptures, intriguing. Paul has no problem with encouraging the churches to present their requests to God.[1] Yet when Paul himself prays for them, his primary focus is not for their challenges, but for the deepening of their relationship with God.

If there were difficulties between distinct groups in the Ephesian church, Paul would be warranted in spending time in his letter praying for those groups to be united. Instead, he asks the Father to strengthen them with power from the Spirit, to fill them with Jesus' love and to give them a deep confidence in that love. The 'to know' (v 19) is not simply awareness of a truth, but closer to the way a spouse deeply knows their partner.

When we come to prayer, there is often a lengthy list of areas in our lives where we want to see God act. Paul's prayer here reminds us that while our God cares for us, provides for us and listens to our requests, he is also a God who wants us to be filled with a deep knowledge that we are loved. We are loved by a God who is always at work, always seeking our good and always acting to bring about his purposes. This is a knowledge that eases our worries and enables us to live with peace, even amid difficulties.

Spend time praying for the quality of your relationship with God. Ask for more understanding of who he is to you and less for what he can do for you.

[1] Phil 4:6

What is the Good Life?

Jesus, you have called me to be formed into your image, along with my brothers and sisters in the church. Help me to embrace that life today.

This can be a difficult passage to understand, but it helps if we remember that this is, fundamentally, a pastoral letter. The first Greek word in chapter 4 is *parakalo,* meaning 'I urge'. This shows that Paul is desperate for the church to live up to its calling, to grow up into Christ (vs 15,16). Paul's theological argument (vs 7–10) serves this point. Jesus, acting with humility and gentleness, with patience and in unity with the Spirit, descended to the earth to defeat those things that held humanity captive, namely sin, death and the devil. When he then ascended to the throne of God, he took captivity with him (v 8, NRSV). This is certainly an odd phrase, but it suggests that Jesus' ascension, the celebration of his victory, was something that would be shared by the freed prisoners. One day, all believers would, in some mysterious way, mature and grow into the whole fullness of Christ.

Paul sets before the Ephesians this glorious vision and he tells them what the path towards it looks like. We are all called to live as Christ lived, with humility and gentleness, patience, bearing with each other in love and making efforts toward unity. Christ has given the church gifts of different people to equip the church for this calling. The apostles, prophets, evangelists, pastors and teachers are not the pinnacle of the Christian life: they are servants of Christ, called to help the church be built up.

The good life, therefore, is not glamorous by the norms of culture, but by God's economy. The servants are not overlooked but celebrated, the humble are not ignored but raised with Christ. The church is beautiful in its display of hard-fought, loving unity, not fame and fortune.

Paul calls us to reorient our lives around God's vision for his church. Reflect on where the health of the body of Christ fits with the rhythms of your life.

BIBLE IN A YEAR: **Numbers 2,3; Matthew 14**

Time to Renew

Holy Spirit, lead me in the ways of Jesus. Make the new self, which God has created, a reality I live in each moment of today.

Healthy theology is practical, it makes a difference every day. There is little value in fathoming the depths of God's character if it doesn't change how we live or love. Paul wrote earlier about the marvel of the new humanity that God has created in Christ Jesus.[1] Now, he unpacks what it looks like to display this new humanity, this new creation, to the world.

He reminds us that there is another way to live, our old way. We can find it so easy to slip into ways of thinking or acting which are unaffected by Jesus. I did not grow up in a relationship with Jesus, so I have lots of ways of thinking and acting that I learned apart from him. Paul reminds me that God has acted to renew the spirit of my mind – and yours too. Paul uses the analogy of clothing to describe what it looks like to live for God. When you get dressed in the morning, you need to select what you will wear and how you will present yourself during the day. God has given you a new wardrobe. We show off these 'new clothes' in how we act towards other people.

Treating people differently, as a Christian, is always a choice, but it is a choice which the Spirit helps us with. The first time we decide to forgive someone who has wronged us or to honour someone who has been shamed can be extremely hard. It is a big choice to make. As we develop our relationship with the Spirit and as he works in our minds, our choices become increasingly aligned with the Spirit's. We find it more natural to wear the clothes of holiness and righteousness which God has given us.

Make a list of old ways you want to put off and new ways you want to put on. Pray and ask the Spirit for help with this.

[1] Eph 2:15

BIBLE IN A YEAR: **Numbers 4,5; Matthew 15**

Ephesians 4:25 – 5:2

Following the Way

Jesus, you call me to follow you, to trust you for my salvation and to live as you lived. Empower me with your Spirit for this today.

The call of Jesus is not to agree with a certain philosophy, to follow a rigid ethical code or to respond to a prophetic summons. The call of Jesus is to follow him, the person we see revealed in the Gospels and the ongoing activity of Christ in our lives and the world today. We follow, not as employees or disregarded slaves, but as beloved children in God's family. In your family, what characteristics or traditions were there? Maybe it was reverence for the elderly, places you visited or meals you ate on particular days. God's family is to be known for truth, unity, peace, honesty, purity, encouragement, kindness, forgiveness and compassion.

That list sounds wonderful, but we can be all too aware of the times we or others fall short of that ideal. We need to make sure that we do not miss a key element in this text, the role of the Holy Spirit. Placing our faith in Christ is not a momentary action, something we do once and then we are left to our own devices to try and be a better person by sheer willpower. When we receive Christ, we receive the Holy Spirit[1] and this means God's power is immediately at work in our hearts and minds to bring about transformation. The question for us is: do we partner with the Spirit or grieve the Spirit?

God's gift of his Spirit is remarkable because the relationship into which we are invited is a truly intimate one. Through our actions and choices, we can celebrate the Spirit's presence, or we can grieve the Spirit. Over time, as we cultivate a relationship with the Spirit, it is as though our spirit is increasingly saturated with the Holy Spirit, as our thoughts and actions become more aligned with those of Jesus.

Spend time praying to the Spirit and enjoying his presence with you. Thank him for being the ever-present counsellor.

---

[1] Eph 1:13

BIBLE IN A YEAR: **Numbers 6,7; Psalms 26,27**

Stark Reminders

Father, as I come before you, reveal to me where I am still living in darkness of thought or action. Please shine your light of love on me.

Paul exhorts the church in Ephesus to live wisely, not unwisely (v 15). When we read wisdom literature in Scripture, such as Proverbs or even the letter from James, it presents us with a stark choice between two ways of living. Will we take the path leading to life or the path that is filled with darkness? This style of writing is blunt and we may not be used to it. We must recognise that wisdom is not about being given a moralistic telling-off, like a naughty child in a classroom. Wisdom comes from someone who puts their arm around our shoulders to speak hard but necessary truths. Wisdom, therefore, only comes from someone who loves us deeply enough to challenge us.

Paul's words here should challenge us, but they do so out of love. We are called away from immoral, impure and improper actions and thoughts, not to try and get right with God but because we already are God's beloved. In a similar vein, the call to a new way of living is not born out of our energies alone, but by being filled continually with the Spirit.

The verb for 'be filled' (v 18) with the Spirit is a continuous verb in Greek. This does not translate easily into the English language, but a good way of understanding this is 'be filled with the Spirit, again and again and again'. When we are confronted with the reality of our sin, Paul encourages us to ask the Spirit to make his presence known to us afresh and for Christians to speak truth and encouragement to each other. We are to saturate ourselves in the songs and psalms of God, as well as with the presence of God himself.

Ask the Spirit for a fresh filling of his presence today. Spend time with music and with others, expressing praises to God.

BIBLE IN A YEAR: **Numbers 8,9; Matthew 16**

Psalm 128

A New Family

Thank you, my brother Jesus, that you have saved me into the family of my Father, with the brothers and sisters of faith beside me.

In the Old Testament, the blessings of God were understood to be a long life, wealth and children, especially male offspring. A decent and honourable burial would be the way a good life was completed. Walking in obedience to God would result in blessings such as these.[1] This is the lens we need to understand this psalm.

At the same time, we should remember that we read the psalm today with the knowledge of the coming of Jesus. His coming has transformed the way we are to view family, prosperity and the blessings of obedience. Whether or not we have a spouse and children of our own, we are now found in an eternal family, the family of those who do the will of God.[2] Whether we are rich or poor, we have the prosperity of knowing Christ and the inheritance of a new heaven and earth.[3] This does not mean that biological children or material prosperity are no longer blessings, but they are not the ultimate signs of a blessed life.

Fear of the Lord is twice revealed as a blessing in this psalm (vs 1,4). Before we determine our blessings by the number of our children, the money we have access to or the length of years we have lived, we need to ask: do we fear the Lord? Do we acknowledge his majesty and give him glory? One day, we are promised, we will be raised and we shall see Jesus, face to face.[4] This does not diminish our hopes and dreams for this life, but it reminds us that they are not our final hope. The blessing that awaits us is a multitude no one can count, worshipping the risen Lamb.[5]

Tell God what you long and dream for, and be honest with him. Then take time to praise him for who he is and his promises to us.

---

[1] Deut 28:1-14 [2] Mark 3:31-35 [3] Eph 1:14 [4] 1 John 3:2 [5] Rev 7:9,10

BIBLE IN A YEAR: **Numbers 10,11; Matthew 17**

Households of Service

Jesus Christ, you gave yourself for me, help me to live a life of love and service to others, pursuing their flourishing as you pursue mine.

Across the world, this text is understood in different ways, depending on the culture it is received in. Some see it as a text of repression and others as a text of liberation and empowerment. Why is this? It is because we always receive and understand the Bible in our context. Our context itself has rules about which things are permissible and which are not. In Paul's day, this letter was received in a context where wives had little power to decide about their futures, whom they married, how money was spent or what decisions were taken in the family. It was a culture where men held much of the power and wives were often viewed as little more than property.

In that context, Paul's words are revolutionary. What might shock you in your culture, is not what shocked the original audience. Paul's words that a wife should submit to her husband were the norm in his day and maybe they still are where you live. What was radical was Paul's instructions to husbands to lay themselves down for their wives. Husbands were not to view their wives simply as property or means for a male offspring, but as women to be loved, cherished, supported and invested in.

There is much benefit to be found in the deep theological study of this passage. It must always, however, lead to marriages built upon the principle of the husband and wife seeking the spiritual flourishing of their spouse. The foundation for this is the reality of Christ and his bride, the church. He has given himself for us and loved us as himself. In return, we give him our devotion. Our marriages should reflect this reality, even if only as a pale shadow.

If you are married, how can you spiritually invest in your spouse? If you are not, pray for the married couples you know that they may flourish in Christ.

BIBLE IN A YEAR: **Numbers 12–14; Psalms 28,29**

Ephesians 6:1–9

It is Not About Your Boss

Father, we pray for the liberation of every person who lives in slavery today. Bring your jubilee of freedom across the face of the earth.

Many times I have heard it said that the best way to understand Paul's words about slavery is to think of the modern workplace, so the text becomes about respecting your boss or treating your workers fairly. In the ancient world, slavery was common, as being employed is common today, but to compare the two in any way beyond this is wrong. Slavery meant you were owned by someone else, that your body was not yours and that you were not able to decide for yourself. This text should not be misused either to downplay the evil of slavery or, as has historically been the case, to support its horrors.

Many ask, why did Paul not simply condemn slavery? This is a valid question and one we must wrestle with. While we may wish Paul had done so, we must recognise that what he did say would have challenged the very fabric of the slave-master relationship in his time. He reminds the slave owners that they also have a master, God himself – and he shows no favouritism. While in this life, one may be a slave or may be a master, God will ultimately act to bring an end to this unjust system. Our question is: do we perpetuate or undermine systems of slavery today?

This is no small question. There is no simple or easy answer. One thing we can take from this passage is that the Lord of heaven and earth sees and knows both the slave and the slave owner. Just as God met the slave girl Hagar in the wilderness and she was allowed to name him as 'the God who sees me',[1] and just as the slave boy Onesimus became a beloved brother,[2] so God is with the oppressed today and he acts to bring freedom, not oppression.

Spend time praying for the enslaved of this world and ask the Father to make us agents of liberation.

---

[1] Gen 16:13 [2] Phlm 16

BIBLE IN A YEAR: **Numbers 15,16; Matthew 18**

What is our Goal?

Heavenly Father, help me to be a faithful witness to Christ, a loving brother or sister in the church and committed to the way of prayer.

After everything Paul has written, he ends with an amazing picture of what the Christian looks like in the spiritual realm. The armour of God reflects the blessings of God with which Paul began his letter. We are kitted out with truth, righteousness, faith and salvation. With this as our clothing, you might expect that Paul would want the Christian to be advancing, taking ground and fighting for God, but that is not the picture he paints. The church is engaged in a struggle with evil powers, unseen but active in the heavenly realms. The role of the church is to remain faithful to God.

We are to be hopeful and expectant that God's kingdom will advance and that salvation will come to all corners of the world. The Christian faith is optimistic about the future, as Jesus will return to restore all things. At the same time, we need to recognise the reality that in a broken world one of the hardest things to do is to remain faithful to Christ throughout our lives, in seasons of ease and celebration and those of difficulty and pain. We are to be like the steadfast tree of Psalm 1, planted by the streams of water, which is the rule and reign of God. We need to be constantly drawing on that refreshing source of life.

Paul's picture is a reminder that we can do something each day to draw close to him. A friend of mine once told me that they would stand in front of a mirror and act out putting on this armour while praying for God to make each item a reality in their mind and heart. These are not just words Paul writes, they are the true status we have before the Father, the identity we live in each day.

Act out placing the armour on and pray for the Spirit of God to impress these truths on your mind and inner being.

BIBLE IN A YEAR: **Numbers 17–19; Matthew 19**

Scripture Union

A BRAND NEW SCRIPTURE UNION HOLIDAY CLUB!

Grab your snorkel and plunge into the book of Matthew with *Deep Sea Divers!*

Deep Sea Divers

Includes photocopiable resources and FREE EXTRAS online

A Scripture Union holiday club programme Great new ideas inspired by experience

Discover the depths of Jesus' love as you dive into his life, death and resurrection with children and young people.

FIND YOUR COPY AT: WWW.SU.ORG.UK/DEEPSEA

Also available at your local Christian bookshop

THE WEEK THAT CHANGED THE WORLD

The first readers of (or listeners to) Mark's Gospel didn't have the luxury of four Gospels to compare with each other. For the largely Gentile audience, probably living in Rome, this was the first organised account of the life, death and resurrection of Jesus. It reads like a series of video shorts, actions taking priority over words, deeds over teaching. Based on the experience of Peter, there's a first-hand vividness to the Gospel. It's frank and honest, particularly in relation to the highs and lows of Peter's role, but with Jesus central to every episode.

Chapters 11 to 16 of Mark encompass the final phase of the account. In the earlier chapters we have seen Jesus' early Galilean ministry and the enigmatic excursions into northern Palestine. The disciples have been called and trained. Everything then hinges on Peter's confession in chapter 8, the recognition that Jesus is the promised Messiah. From this point on, the direction of the action turns south towards Jerusalem, with the departure from Galilee. The men and women from the north approach the capital.

Chapters 1 to 10 of the Gospel have been selective, covering three years of Jesus' ministry. They read like the edited highlights of an eventful time. By contrast, chapters 11 to 16 give a day by day, often hour by hour, account of a single week. Miracles are few. Instead, it's a time of controversies, some initiated by Jesus, others the work of the religious and legal authorities, threatened by the powerful presence of Jesus in a city already overcrowded by the influx of pilgrims for the Passover festival. The climax is devastating, an abyss of injustice, torture and death quietly transformed in a garden early one morning. Just as Jesus said it would.

Brian Radcliffe

Mark 11:1–11

The Banner Man

Invite God to open up a familiar story in a new and striking way.

In the month of October 1936, two hundred men marched from the north-east of England to London, the capital city and centre of power. Their purpose was to highlight poverty and unemployment in the former shipbuilding town of Jarrow. Today's reading presents us with a man, driven by a clear but different sense of purpose, together with his ragtag group of followers (women as well as men). They are entering the city of Jerusalem, the centre of religious and political power, at the end of their journey from Galilee. Read again Mark 10:32–34 to remind yourself of Jesus' driven agenda and the mixed emotions of those with him.

Jesus is the master of understatement. On the one hand he overtly assumes the role of the Messiah, the Son of Man, the one who is to bring God's salvation to the nation of Israel. Yet he demonstrates this in the humblest fashion. Fulfilling the prophecy of Zechariah 9:9, he enters the city on a colt. He isn't the firebrand, but calmly challenges the status quo by his entry. He accepts the traditional greeting of 'Hosanna', given to every pilgrim up for the Passover festival. However, he evokes something more. The cloaks and branches spread on the ground signify homage, a gradual recognition that Jesus is someone of very special significance.

What is understood about this entrance by those who accompanied Jesus on his journey south, by those who witnessed his arrival, by you? The revelation is gradual. Enough is enough, for one day. Jesus takes a leisurely look around the Temple courts. He then seeks accommodation at Bethany.

Listen to 'The Banner Man' by Blue Mink (available on streaming channels and YouTube). Let the exuberance of the music recreate the entry into Jerusalem. Join in the Hosannas.

BIBLE IN A YEAR: **Numbers 20,21; Matthew 20**

Clearing the Decks

Make a mental list of acquaintances you will meet (or have met) today. Invite the Holy Spirit to move in their lives.

Verses 12–14 provide us with a conundrum. Are we seeing the human side of Jesus: a disturbed night of moral indignation at what he'd seen at the Temple; breakfast not up to much; an early morning? We can't help feeling a little sympathy for the fig tree.

The Court of the Gentiles was the outermost court of the Temple at Jerusalem. Unlike the inner courts, it was accessible to Jews and non-Jews alike. It was also a handy short cut from the city to the Mount of Olives. The market was here, providing wine, oil, salt and birds for Temple rituals, along with facilities for currency exchange from Roman and Greek to the Jewish coinage required for offerings. So far, so good. However, many of the stalls were owned by the high priest, exchange rates were sky high and profiteering was rife. Jesus' anger and violent action is directed at the moral cesspit, the secularisation created in this, the only area of the Temple where 'all nations' were allowed to gather for prayer.[1] This court was deemed inclusive rather than exclusive, yet the spirituality on display left everything to be desired.

In contrast to the previous day's humble and self-effacing acceptance of his Messianic role, Jesus has now engaged in a public confrontation with the religious hierarchy of the city. The public reaction is amazement. Who would dare to oppose those in control of the Temple like this? The authorities' reaction is to silence him – but they recognise in Jesus a power they cannot control. Furthermore, he is drawing public support to himself and away from them. They cannot afford to let this happen.

How much do our acquaintances know about our faith? Do we have a secularised outer ring to our relationships that is untouched by the words of Jesus?

[1] Isa 56:7

BIBLE IN A YEAR: **Numbers 22,23; Psalm 30**

Mark 11:20–33

Who's Boss?

What are my plans for today? What's my motivation? How will I achieve them?

Authority is the key word for Day 3 in Jerusalem. Who has the right and the power to take decisive action in the Temple precincts? It's a key issue for the Sanhedrin, who are responsible for the policing of the Temple courts. They cannot ignore Jesus' cavalier action of the previous day. It undermines their authority. It's a law-and-order issue.

Jesus' response is subtle. First, he has prepared the ground for the Sanhedrin's question, by the incident with the fig tree. Peter draws everyone's attention to the withered remains of yesterday's growing tree (v 21). Jesus' teaching about faith in prayer begins with the authority behind a believer's faith: 'Have faith in God' (v 22). By implication, that's the source of Jesus' own authority in dealing with the sorry fig tree. Second, when challenged by the Sanhedrin, Jesus turns the issue into a classic rabbinic debate. Unlike his opponents, Jesus isn't attached to an authorised rabbinic school. Nor was John the Baptist. So where did John's authority come from? If the Sanhedrin reply that it came from God, Jesus' response would be to question their doubts about John. If the Sanhedrin reply that it was no more than John's strength of personality then… verse 32b gives us the answer.

There are times when our thoughts, words and actions can appear countercultural to those who don't share our beliefs. For instance, wealth, integrity, gender and the sanctity of life are live issues. So what is our authority for expressing these views? Our faith is to be rooted and grounded in God, not our own bias, nurture, social constructs or popular philosophy.

When our faith is wavering, whom do we fear? Is it self-doubt, public acceptance or unresolved guilt that compromises our authority? Pray for Bible-based, Spirit-filled clarity.

BIBLE IN A YEAR: **Numbers 24,25; Matthew 21**

Dry Grass

Forgive me my wrongs, as I forgive those who wrong me.

Living roofs have become something of a fashion among conservation-minded folk. Instead of a slate or stone covering to a building, there is a layer of growing medium, planted with grasses, sedums and wild flowers. A living roof is beneficial to wildlife, aids water runoff management and is good insulation. However, it does have its drawbacks. Because the growing medium is shallow, it dries out very easily (does this remind you of a parable Jesus told?) and the plants die. Also, it's no use for growing the year's vegetable crop, as the roots cannot develop.

This psalm is one of the series known as 'Songs of Ascent', probably sung by pilgrims entering Jerusalem for one of the festivals, such as Passover, or climbing the steps to the Temple. First, it gives a highly truncated version of the oppressed history of the nation of Israel, ending with a triumphant celebration of their freedom, delivered by a righteous God. Then it's the turn of those who doled out the oppression. The psalm compares them to that grass on the roof. They are shameful and beyond reckoning (v 5), transient (v 6), non-productive (v 7) and friendless (v 8).

How do we respond to those who cause us worry, stress and pain? The psalms frequently hold nothing back in their demands for justice and revenge. This is a perfect example. Jesus gives a modified, maybe more constructive, approach: 'love your enemies and pray for those who persecute you'.[1] Rather than annihilation, our hope is for transformation.

Think of three people with whom you have relationship problems. Pray for them in an honest way, acknowledging the issues and praying for them in a way which benefits them.

---

[1] Matt 5:44

BIBLE IN A YEAR: **Numbers 26,27; Matthew 22**

Mark 12:1–12

If the Cap Fits...

Lord, open my mind and my imagination, that I might understand and apply all that you might speak to me.

The old stories are the best. Jesus' audience, both scholars and ordinary people, would recognise his reworking of the well-known 'Song of the Vineyard' from Isaiah chapter 5. In the original, there's no avoiding the criticism of the two kingdoms of Israel and Judah. The priests and teachers of the Sanhedrin in Jesus' day would probably acknowledge the mistakes of these past generations. But Jesus takes the parable a stage further. Isaiah's owner friend, who built the vineyard, is a clear symbol for God himself. Rather than reaping a crop of sour grapes and rewilding the land, the owner sends his servants to claim his share of the harvest. Past history gathers pace down the generations, arriving at the character of the son. Without overtly identifying himself with this character, Jesus paints a picture of what he knows is about to take place.

How long does it take for the penny to drop with the Jewish leaders? At what point do they realise that they are approaching their last chance? As they turn against him, Jesus delivers the devastating conclusion: if they reject him, they are rejecting the stone described in Psalm 118:22, the most important of all. Layer by layer, Jesus strips off any doubts they may have about him. He is the promised Messiah. The problem is that he's not what they expected.

What are our expectations whenever we turn to Scripture or meet God in prayer? The wonder is that, like in any relationship, there's always a new dimension to discover. How then do we respond, especially if it's not what we expected?

Imagine yourself as that vineyard, entrusted to you by the owner. What has the yield been like? Thank God that, as we offer him his due, he lovingly accepts it.

BIBLE IN A YEAR: **Numbers 28,29; Psalm 31**

Question Time

Shield me, Lord, from irrelevant concerns. What is on *your* mind?

It's just like questioning the prime minister in the UK House of Commons. Earlier the opposition quizzed Jesus on a domestic issue, the authority of John the Baptist. Next, an obsequious politician poses a question about relations with the occupying power, the Romans. The motives behind the questions are so similar. The Pharisees and Herodians are attempting to catch Jesus out (v 13). The intention is to compromise Jesus. Will he upset Jewish nationalists by endorsing Roman rule? Will he upset the Roman authorities by denying the primacy of their currency?

Spotting the tactic being employed, Jesus drags the debate into the real world. 'Bring me a denarius' (v 15) (let's get down to the nuts and bolts). The coin is simply a symbol of the machinery of state. It's no big deal. It's the way society works (and in many ways Roman rule gave Palestine a significant measure of stability). The big deal is what we give to God.

Paul later explored the same issue.[1] A society that is stable politically and economically is to be respected and honoured, because God is the source of such stability. Law and order, justice and equality flow from him. However, what about when we sense injustice and inequality in the decisions of our government? What about when we sense that the government is doing wrong rather than doing right in God's eyes? Sometimes unfortunately that's the way society works. In the real world that's when we address the big deal, what we give to God may overrule our political allegiances.

Choose three current political issues. What appear to be the motives of the authorities? How do these sit side by side with what you believe to be God's agenda?

---

[1] Rom 13:1–7

BIBLE IN A YEAR: **Numbers 30,31; Matthew 23**

Mark 12:18–27

Back to the Book

May our understanding and application of today's scripture equip us for the day laid before us.

Like a wrestling tag team, the next set of opponents is brought on, attempting to bring Jesus to the floor. The tale of a woman seven times widowed becomes increasingly ludicrous as it develops. One can sense the crowd joining in as bereavement is piled upon bereavement, culminating in the apparently decisive, unanswerable question, 'whose wife will she be … ?' (v 23). The Sadducees are the unlikely proponents of this attack. On the one hand, they're not normally allies of the more progressive Pharisees who preceded them. On the other hand, they're described as denying the concept of a resurrection (v 18) – yet their question is about relationships in the afterlife.

The Sadducees' starting point is Scripture: Mosaic Law outlines such a situation in relation to two brothers.[1] To tangle Jesus in the detail, they present a caricature of this teaching. A simple, practical application for life in a developing nation has become the basis for an intellectual argument. Jesus' response tackles the Sadducees' initial premise: 'you do not know the Scriptures or the power of God' (v 24).

It's not difficult to abuse the Bible. When we identify proof texts to support our pet biases without regard for the more complex bigger picture, we're abusing the Bible. When we parrot familiar verses of praise rather than voicing our true feelings, we're abusing the Bible. When we avoid difficult sections, we're abusing the Bible. When we over-contextualise teaching and deem it irrelevant to the modern day, we're abusing the Bible. The power of God to apply Scripture to our daily lives is what matters most.

Read a chapter of Deuteronomy (15, 24 or 26, perhaps), in the context of a plan for a young nation. Invite the Spirit to draw parallels with your own life.

---

[1] Deut 25:5

The Planes of Love

As I read your Word, may I look first to you and then to the world in which I live.

My grandson loves lists: 'Grandad, what are your top three fizzy drinks/footballers/curries?' Similarly, the radio programme *Desert Island Discs* asks which eight recordings we would take with us if cast away on a desert island. We like to know what's important to other people. This teacher asks Jesus for his Number 1 commandment. In reply, he receives the additional bonus of Number 2.

Jesus' response is initially conventional. He quotes the Shemah creed that every pious Jew would recite daily (with the addition of 'mind').[1] Our total being, emotions, spirit, intellect and body, is to be employed in loving the one God. Everything we think, speak and do is to bring pleasure to him. This is love on the vertical plane, love that ascends to the God who has created and sustained us. Then Jesus flips the direction by 90 degrees. He adds a quote from Leviticus, directing the love outwards on a horizontal plane to those around us.[2] We are commanded to show no less regard for those we live, work and play with than we would show to ourselves.

There's been interest in the media recently about the topic of altruism, looking to the needs of others before our own. This is a healthy development, a countercultural offensive against consumerism, and is worthy of commendation. Yet I'd suggest that this movement's horizons are restricted. If the good I do stems only from my worldview and my resources, then whatever I can achieve has its limits. To look to God first is to open up the needs of our world to the limitless wisdom and resources of the one, true God. As Paul says, 'How great are God's riches ... All glory to him for ever.'[3]

Draw down the limitless love of God into a situation you feel powerless to address on your own.

[1] Deut 6:4,5 [2] Lev 19:18b [3] See Rom 11:33–36, NLT

BIBLE IN A YEAR: **Numbers 34,35; Matthew 25**

Mark 12:35–44

Watch Words

'May these words of my mouth and this meditation of my heart be pleasing in your sight, Lord, my Rock and my Redeemer.'[1]

'All the world's a stage', wrote Shakespeare in his comedy, *As You Like it*. Take today, for example. Did we deliberately choose the clothes we're wearing, in order to project an image, like an actor's costume? Have we carefully chosen the words we've spoken and the actions we've made, so as to control the reactions of those who've been watching us? For many of us, to a greater or lesser extent, there has been an element of performance, if we're honest. So it is, Jesus says, with the teachers of the Law. They wear their costume, take the dominant position and make the carefully worded speeches, all for a show (v 40). Watch them, but watch out!

A similar drama unfolds as Jesus watches a crowd scene, where offerings are made into the Temple treasury. Extravagant actions are displayed, as large sums are deposited by those who can afford it. The money is thrown in, all for show. Then, by contrast, two small coins are slipped in by a poor widow. The action is hardly noticed. She's probably embarrassed, not a scene stealer. Quite the opposite in fact.

Calling his disciples out of the large crowd to him, Jesus teaches that in the kingdom of God money has no value of itself. The motives for the actions of those who are offering is what matters. Motive and opportunity. For those who are rich, their offering is merely a contribution. There is more where that came from. For the poor widow, her offering is a sacrifice. She returns to an empty home with an empty stomach.

Take a look at your motives for giving to church and to charity. How much is duty and how much is out of love?

---

[1] Ps 19:14

BIBLE IN A YEAR: **Numbers 36; Deuteronomy 1; Psalm 32**

A Private Word

Lord, come into a world that is stressed and strained, broken yet breaking more. Bring me reassurance that you are still in control.

Many times I've stood in front of a building and marvelled at its design, construction and artistry. So it is with the unnamed disciple looking back at the Jerusalem Temple, a wonder of the Roman world and a symbol of God's presence with his people. Jesus' enigmatic comment on the building's total destruction comes as a jolt in more senses than one. Later, an explanation is requested by Jesus' closest quartet.

In reply, Jesus paints a picture of a world of imposters, wars, natural disasters, hostility, persecution and family betrayal. Sandwiched in between these stark disclosures are words of encouragement: 'do not be alarmed' (v 7), 'the beginning of birth-pains' (v 8), 'do not worry' (v 11), 'it is not you speaking, but the Holy Spirit' (v 11). Finally, there is the mind-blowing (to an orthodox Jew) revelation that the gospel will be preached to all nations.

Even the despised Gentiles will be given the opportunity to enter the fold. Yes, there is a hazardous world to come, Jesus says, but God's hand is present. He will not desert his people.

For the early readers of Mark's Gospel, the picture painted by Jesus matched their experience. The siege and destruction of Jerusalem in AD 70 would have been fresh in their minds. For many readers, the reality of wars, natural disasters and persecution during the reigns of the emperors Claudius and Nero were vivid memories, if not present events. God, however, will not desert his people. To us, as we read about the world news – war, climate change, bogus Messiahs (political and religious) and a fragmented society – the message is the same: God will not desert his people.

Paul expands Jesus' image of childbirth.[1] It's painful, it's messy, it's chaotic – but the birth is promised. God will bring in his kingdom. Grasp the hope!

[1] Rom 8:22

BIBLE IN A YEAR: **Deuteronomy 2,3; Matthew 26**

Odd One Out

May I take my time, unhurried, as I read your Word.

As a former literature teacher, I like to explore the structure of a piece of writing. In this 'Song of Ascents', we have three pairs of verses, the second verse of each pair echoing the first. Verses 1 and 2 are a desperate plea to be heard. Verses 5 and 6 have the theme of wait … wait … wait … wait. Verses 7 and 8 bring the reassuring news that redemption comes from God's love. What of verses 3 and 4, though? Here, instead of an echo, there is a dramatic contrast. Verse 3 paints a stark picture of humanity's sinful nature, barring us from relationship with God, whereas verse 4 reveals the wonder of forgiveness offered to us, so we might not merely stand in God's presence, but are allowed to be part of his team.

From our kitchen there is a perfect view of sunrise over the Staffordshire Moorlands. Usually I wake at about 7am and make a pot of coffee. In summer, that's too late to enjoy the sunrise. In winter I often sit in the darkness, waiting for the first glow over Axe Edge. In late December it feels like I'm waiting for ever – but it always happens. There's no day when the sun doesn't rise.

Now I can sense a different flow to this psalm. I recognise my failings all too easily (vs 1,2). I know the theological truth of God's forgiveness (vs 3,4). Yet it doesn't necessarily come immediately (vs 5,6). I sometimes have to wait, if I am fully to experience God's work in me. My hope, however, is positive and active, because I know it will happen, just as the sun always rises. When it happens, unfailing and fully (v 7), I can do nothing but exhort you to try it (vs 7,8).

Do you have a long-repeated prayer for which you'd love an answer? In the light of God's unfailing love and full redemption, bring it once more to him.

BIBLE IN A YEAR: **Deuteronomy 4,5; Matthew 27**

This is What You Know

Father, I invite your Spirit to make clear to me the message you have for me today.

I admit there is much I don't understand about this passage. What is historical prophecy about specific events and what is more general symbolic prophecy about the second coming of Jesus? Who are 'the elect, whom he has chosen' (v 20)? Which generation 'will certainly not pass away until all these things have happened' (v 30)? Clearly, Jesus is warning his followers about events to come within their lifetime (with a nod from the writer to the early audience who remember these taking place; v 14). But what is here for me, today?

First, there is the sense that God works beyond our limited concept of chronological time. Jesus initially foretells events that have yet to happen, out of concern for his followers (v 23b). Cut to the end days when the Son of Man returns 'with great power and glory' (v 26). There is a huge gap. Second, as in yesterday's passage, the overriding message is of reassurance. However bad life might seem, God is ultimately in control. Over the centuries of a world seemingly out of control, this is God's promise. He will not desert his beloved people. To me, that is a great relief!

So how, in the twenty-first century, do we live? Jesus relates a simple country parable about a fig tree. It's about reading the signs of the times. New buds, even in the middle of a snowstorm, mean that summer isn't far away. Summer always arrives. Even the bad times are good if they're a sign that we're a stage nearer the return of Jesus.

Buds signify the end of winter and the coming of spring: light after darkness, new life after apparent death. The coming of Jesus brings light, healing and new life.

BIBLE IN A YEAR: **Deuteronomy 6,7; Psalm 33**

Mark 13:32–37

Don't be Caught Out

Look at your to-do list for today. What are you hoping for, fearing, anticipating and ready for?

I need to look at my diary every morning. It's important to me that I have some idea of the shape of events for the coming day, because I'm not very good at improvising. Surprises make me panic, freeze or respond in an inappropriate fashion. I so wish I could make a note of 'that day or hour' (v 32) Jesus talks of, when we shall see 'the Son of Man coming in clouds with great power and glory' (v 26). I'd be ready, dressed in my best, Bible in one hand, the other raised in worship. I really would, if the date was in my diary. But that's not how it will be.

In a short parable similar to that of the talents,[1] Jesus describes the life of a believer as one of ceaseless vigilance. However, he doesn't mean a life lived on the edge of panic. Instead, it's a life in which we fulfil our necessary daily responsibilities, not just in practical terms but in spiritual terms. If we require a template for this, maybe a look back at the reading on 14 March ('The Planes of Love') would be in order.[2] To love God and to love our neighbours as ourselves day by day is what the 'owner of the house' (v 35) requires.

The importance of maintaining this vigilance is shown by the three imperatives Jesus uses: 'Be on guard! Be alert!' (v 33); 'Watch!' (v 37). (Squirrel these requirements away until we meet them again in the Garden of Gethsemane.) Before we, as onlookers, begin to make judgements on the four disciples who are present on both occasions, take note of Jesus' final words – this applies to everyone! A sombre yet thrilling thought as we accompany them back down from the Mount of Olives.

Pray for the doorkeepers. Church leaders often feel responsible for the whole house. Pray that this burden may be light and that they too may receive your neighbourly love.

---

[1] Matt 25:14–30; Luke 19:11–27 [2] Mark 12:28–34

BIBLE IN A YEAR: **Deuteronomy 8,9; Matthew 28**

Relative Values

'What can I give him, poor as I am?'[1] Bring your day, your community and yourself as an offering to God.

'It's all about the timing', as the comedian said – but this is no laughing matter. For the Jewish authorities, the arrest of Jesus and his subsequent death could not be delayed much longer. The threat he represented to the whole of the Sanhedrin was reaching tipping point. 'But not during the festival' (v 2). Why? Secrecy and the right timing for the arrest were important because the city was teeming with crowds and Jesus' public popularity was clearly evident.

Meanwhile, in a village just outside the city a private event takes place, one that has far-reaching consequences. A woman interrupts a meal for Jesus and his followers. Was she a gatecrasher or one of the party? More significant is what she does and the value of the perfume with which she anoints the head of Jesus, an act of pure devotion and worship.

There is bickering around the table, 'more than a year's wages', 'money given to the poor' (v 5). The reactions have a ring of indignant moral superiority. By contrast, Jesus' reaction is to jump to the woman's defence. Rather than giving a rebuke, he describes her act of anointing him as a thing of beauty. It is worship in its purest form, a prophetic act, both foretelling and preparing him for his imminent death and burial. Seizing the opportunity, she has painted the clearest picture of Jesus' mission. It's a memorable moment.

Her 'inappropriate' use of a valuable luxury and Jesus' commendation of what she's done are enough to persuade Judas into making a critical decision, to hand Jesus over and provoke the final act of the confrontation.

To Jesus, the widow's 'small copper coins'[2] and this woman's perfume are both priceless. By contrast, the fee paid to Judas is worthless. So – what can I give him?

[1] Christina Rossetti, 1830–94, 'In the bleak midwinter' [2] Mark 12:42

BIBLE IN A YEAR: **Deuteronomy 10,11; Romans 1**

Mark 14:12–26

Surely You Don't Mean Me?

Father, engage my mind and my imagination as I read your Word.

Who'd be on your guest list for a celebration meal? I'd like to choose Bono from U2, Jurgen Klopp, Nicole Kidman, Stormzy, athlete Christine Ohurogu and Bear Grylls. A mixed bunch, you may say, but every one is a believer in Jesus Christ. My guests would be no more of a mixed bunch than those twelve who shared the Passover supper with Jesus. Among the guests was a doubter, a pair of ambitious brothers, a blusterer who would let Jesus down and someone who had already initiated a plan to betray him. But every one had responded to Jesus' call to follow him.

It was a bittersweet meal. A celebration of the redemption of the people of God from slavery in Egypt, but with the cloud of Jesus' revelation (v 18) hanging over the festivities. As they shared the bread and drank from the cup, a ritual they'd participated in for many years, each of the twelve would be engaged in self-examination, 'Surely you don't mean me?' (v 19).

Communion, mass, the breaking of bread – this is a familiar institution to us. Paul's teaching in 1 Corinthians 11:23–25, along with his commentary in the rest of the chapter, has formalised what took place. In that room, around a table, looking into his disciples' eyes, Jesus personally identified himself with the loaf broken by his own hands and the wine in the cup. Participation deeply involved each disciple. Passing bread and wine from hand to hand they took, they ate, they drank. Each one was asking, 'Surely you don't mean me?' This week, possibly Thursday of next week, you are likely to share the bread and the cup. Remember that Passover supper and ask yourself what Jesus is thinking as he looks into your eyes, shares the bread, passes the cup.

Strip away the institution, the ceremony. Share a simple meal with Jesus.

BIBLE IN A YEAR: **Deuteronomy 12–14; Romans 2**

Mark 14:27–31

Not me!

Father, open my eyes that I might see clearly the world around me – and myself.

The older we get, the more inclined my wife and I are to criticise the driving habits of other road users. 'She's using a phone', 'He overtook on double white lines', 'Dip your headlights!' Then we realise that, in our distraction, we were driving at 40 miles per hour in a 30 zone. It's just like Jesus' comment about removing the log from our own eye before examining the speck of sawdust in someone else's.[1] So it is with Peter. 'Even if everyone else fails you, I won't', he declares with bravado (see v 29). We'll leave his dramatic failure until later.

Emotions are running high among the disciples. Jesus has just revealed that there is a traitor among them. Now he declares that they will all, every one of them, let him down. As they walk towards the Mount of Olives, the bond of trust within the group broken down, Peter impetuously voices what the others want to say. Mark gives us a warts-and-all portrait of the man whose recollections lay behind his Gospel. At this moment Peter, no doubt, believed in his own courage. So did the others (v 31). Jesus knew them better.

In the heat of the moment, we can be tempted to say it like it is. I have been known to do so, and at such times I totally believed in the right of what I said. I felt justified. Jesus knew me better – and he knew the circumstances that would unfold. For Peter and for me there was the necessity to face reality and experience brokenness, before Jesus could rebuild in unexpected ways. The irony of it was that Jesus had already dropped the hint that this was not the end: 'But after I have risen ...' (v 28). However, no one was listening.

In the turmoil of daily life, may we have the wisdom to pause, to listen and to see clearly before we make our responses.

[1] Matt 7:3; Luke 6:41

BIBLE IN A YEAR: **Deuteronomy 15,16; Psalm 34**

Mark 14:32–42

The Reality of Commitment

Father, may my concentration be totally on what you might say to me today through your Word.

My son recently competed in an Ironman event: a swim, bike and running marathon that took between seven and eight hours to complete. His training leading up to the event required many months of hour after hour of gruelling activity in all weathers. I admire his commitment. In contrast, the commitment here of Peter, James and John leaves a lot to be desired. Their task is simple. While Jesus spends time in private prayer, they are to stay a short distance off and to keep watch. Is Jesus aware of the impending arrival of his accusers? Is he testing the disciples' understanding of his earlier words to be on their guard?[1] Whichever the answer, the trio fail completely. Three times Jesus returns to them – to discover that, whatever their good intentions, a big meal, wine and the late hour have conspired to defeat them. They are sound asleep.

Jesus' commitment to the task given him by his Father is total. Not that he doesn't double-check that the way ahead of him is entirely necessary (v 36). In a perfect world he would rather not drink this cup of suffering – but this isn't a perfect world… yet. For Jesus, this is God's heavenly will, enacted on earth, and his commitment to that will must be seen through to its bitter end… and beyond.

My intentions for God are good. I want to do what he knows is best for myself, my family, my community and his world. It's the little things that let me down: a late night, a silly argument, hackles raised at something seen or heard, the attractions that vie for my attention. My commitment may sometimes require sacrifice and dogged determination. But that's when the kingdom comes.

Repeat the words of the Lord's Prayer. When you reach 'Your kingdom come, your will be done', pause and ask what God wants you to be committed to today.

[1] Mark 13:9,23

BIBLE IN A YEAR: **Deuteronomy 17,18; Romans 3**

Having a Laugh

'... **your kingdom come, your will be done, on earth as it is in heaven.'**[1]

I'm a sucker for satirical comedy. I enjoy the way that pertinent comments can puncture the self-opinionated, the pseudo-intellectual, the purveyor of contradictory political statements. I often laugh out loud and am reassured that truth will out. God laughs (v 4) at the pathetic attempts by rulers throughout the world to throw off his just, true and wise structures (v 3). God's laughter, his derision, builds into rebuke (v 5a) and terrifying anger (v 5b). His divinely appointed king will show the world's rulers the true way: God's king in God's city (v 6).

This psalm works two ways. On the one hand it inaugurates the rule of King David, one of the world's greatest kings. His reign was a reign of godly relationship (v 7) and of power (v 9). It was the start of a dynasty (v 8). Christians see the dynasty reaching its fulfilment in Jesus. The Father–son relationship between God and King David (v 7) is fulfilled in Jesus; this is illustrated by Mark at Jesus' baptism[2] and his transfiguration[3] and echoed by Peter.[4] Paul outlines the same relationship[5] and it's brought together twice by the writer to the Hebrews.[6] Jesus the Christ is a King in a dynasty that stretches right back to King David.

So how should a ruler, a politician, in the time of King David and today respond to this inauguration? The wise thing to do is to run with it, with some amount of trepidation but celebrating the inherent security (vs 11,12). Would that more politicians of our generation had the good sense to do so!

'Blessed are all who take refuge in him' (v 12). Pray this benediction on family, friends and all whom God brings to mind.

[1] Matt 6:10 [2] Mark 1:11 [3] Mark 9:7 [4] 2 Pet 1:17 [5] Acts 13:33 [6] Heb 1:5; 5:5

BIBLE IN A YEAR: **Deuteronomy 19,20; Romans 4**

Mark 14:43–52

Sealed with a Kiss

Father, be with me as I enter the dark places. May I know the light of your truth.

The onset of anarchy! It's dark in the wooded garden, difficult to pick out who is who. Jesus is emotionally vulnerable, rising from his moment of crisis in communion with his Father (vs 35,36) to discover his isolation from his closest friends, asleep on watch. The rabble, sent to arrest Jesus, appears disorganised, armed with a mixture of improvised weapons. An affectionate kiss becomes the sign of betrayal. There is a mild skirmish, then Jesus is left alone with his betrayer and his accusers. His followers, even the youth who stayed longest, have deserted him.

There is, however, a certain measure of clarity that emerges from the shadows. First, the real perpetrators are obvious. The full authority of the whole Sanhedrin lies behind the rabble (v 43). It may be enacted under the cover of darkness, but this is the moment of decisive attack. Second, the fragile courage of the followers of Jesus is made plain. When push comes to shove they run, after some token resistance. Finally, there is the openness of Jesus. As he points out, he had confronted the authorities in the open (v 49a): they arrested him in the darkness. But this is how it must be (v 49b).

The world we live in is a shadowy place. It's not always clear where right and wrong lie. Often they can appear uneasy bedmates. Sometimes the violent chaos of war, starvation, greed and desire confuses us. Even the good guys can be bad in a crisis. We want to shine as bright lights, but our bulb is rather dimmed by doubt. We long for clarity. Clarity about who and where the enemy is. Clarity about our own limitations and how to put these at God's disposal. Clarity about the power and authority of Jesus. Let's turn on the light.

Jesus brings light[1] and you are to be a light.[2] Shine that light on something that perplexes you at this moment.

---

[1] John 8:12 [2] Matt 5:14–16

BIBLE IN A YEAR: **Deuteronomy 21,22; Psalm 35**

Rough Justice

Father, I follow at a distance (v 54). Draw me closer to you.

This was a gathering outside of Jewish law. An ecclesiastical trial in front of the entire Sanhedrin was not permitted at night. Under cover of darkness, there is one motive behind the expedient bending of the rules: Jesus must be put to death because of the threat he offers to the Jewish establishment. A trail of witnesses, no more coordinated than the rabble that was sent to arrest him, fails to elicit any response from Jesus. There's no need. The slapdash attempt to produce 'evidence' speaks for itself (v 55).

The high priest himself is forced to intervene, eventually asking the crucial question: 'Are you the Messiah … ?' (v 61b). We've arrived at the heart of the matter, the crisis point in this mockery of a trial. Jesus' response, in the affirmative, condemns him by his own words. Caiaphas' dramatic reaction (v 63) seals the verdict. The Sanhedrin, acting in the shadows, foiled by lack of evidence, are successful. Why? Because Jesus speaks the clear, unvarnished truth. He can do no other. It's in his nature.

It's surprising to see the reaction that speaking the truth can provoke. To shine a light on injustice, the abuse of power, perversion and greed in our society can lead to a harsh response. Throughout our world, there are those who are imprisoned, denied basic human rights, some who have died, because they have spoken the truth to power. For many, it's because of their undeniable faith. For others, it's because they've stood up for the values of the kingdom of God, whether overtly or because of their personal conviction. Jesus, like them, beaten, spat on and verbally abused (v 65), receives the undeserved punishment. For him, this is the point of no return.

Read through today's news headlines. Pray for those who are today suffering for speaking truth to power.

BIBLE IN A YEAR: **Deuteronomy 23,24; Romans 5**

WEDNESDAY 27 MARCH
Mark 14:66–72

Shamed

Open my history to me, Lord. May I be honest and realistic before you.

Peter thought he was just one of the crowd, safely hidden in the mass of people who'd gathered for the developing event – but the security camera focuses in on him. First, a servant girl remembers a face. 'You're one of them, aren't you?' she accuses. As soon as he opens his mouth to deny the fact, Peter drops himself in it. You can't mistake a Scouser or a Geordie, or a Galilean accent. The crowd begins to mutter and she accuses him again. Others join in and he's forced to strengthen his denial by playing the foul-mouthed northerner. Presumably the crowd is convinced by this performance, for Peter is allowed to slink away, hear the cock crow's condemnation and break down in shame.

Our downfalls are rarely instantaneous. Peter's began earlier in the day. It started with brash self-confidence (v 29), strongly asserted moments later (v 31). The temptation of sleep (v 37) is followed by the blind panic of flight (v 50). An attempt to sneak into the fringe of the crowd results in identification and this night's total denial. So much is promised but so little delivered. How deep the shame. How could he ever face Jesus again?

In my naivety, I've often promised much to friends, to family and to God. I've sincerely believed in my capabilities, and maybe that's where the problem lies? The person I want to be may not be the person I actually am. Paul put his finger on this fact of human nature,[1] and if it's true for him then it's definitely true for me. Thankfully, forgiveness is to come for Peter, but that's later in the story. Meanwhile, let's honestly face up to who we really are.

Revisit your journey of faith. Remember your naive assertions. Face up to the failures and regrets. Bring them to Jesus so he can look at you with eyes of love.

---

[1] Rom 7:19

BIBLE IN A YEAR: **Deuteronomy 25,26; Romans 6**

Mark 15:1–20

Crowd Control

May the familiar never become mundane. Open your Word to me with a freshness I cannot ignore – and give me courage to face it.

For some, it had been a sleepless night. For Pilate it meant an early summons to address a threat to public order. In turbulent Palestine the risk of riot was always just below the surface. The key to peaceful rule was to appeal to the crowd's immediate interests. The offer to release a terrorist leader, or even Jesus (v 9), would be a small price to pay. The Sanhedrin also knew that the crowd held the power in this political game. Their cunning plan (v 1), fuelled by spurious allegations, was to whip the crowd into a frenzy (v 11), forcing Pilate, against his better judgement (vs 9,10,14,15), to hand Jesus over to the soldiers for crucifixion.

The chemistry of this crowd is a complex social enigma. Are these the same ones who had welcomed Jesus into the capital, recognising him as the Messiah? Or has that crowd fearfully melted into the shadows? Does the Sanhedrin ignite a different group into this orgy of hatred, fired by latent nationalistic undercurrents? Is the riot that the Sanhedrin feared[1] actually their most potent weapon? Can Pilate, the symbol of Roman occupation, be overcome by people power? One thing is certain. In all this, God's divine purposes are being fulfilled. It may not appear so, but he is in control.

I find the violence of verses 16–20 unbearable. For anyone to be flogged, beaten, spat upon and subjected to vicious mockery is beyond my comprehension. It must have been a place of intense loneliness. Yet Jesus, God himself, knowingly followed this route. For me. For you. Don't shrink from this reality. This is part of what it cost for our salvation.

Draw together every image of mindless violence you've witnessed, both fictional and in real life. See Jesus as the victim. Let it penetrate and reduce you to tears.

[1] Mark 14:2

BIBLE IN A YEAR: **Deuteronomy 27,28; Romans 7**

Onlookers or Participants

Take me back, Lord, to this day. May I see, hear, touch, taste and smell the reality of what you've done.

And so we arrive at the turning point of history. The death of God's Son. For us, the heartbreaking breakthrough of a price paid. Yet, for many of those who witnessed it, it was nothing out of the ordinary. Golgotha was a very public place, a through route from here to there. Simon was the unlucky one, a passer-by on his way in from the country, forced into the role of cross-bearer (v 21). Doubtless he shared the insults hurled at Jesus. Soldiers offered Jesus the routine sedative, then shared out the spoils, as usual. Mockery heaped on mockery from those on their way to market, or maybe (ironically) to the Temple, at the assumed charlatan, found out for who he was (vs 29–32). Even fellow criminals joined in with their dying breath (v 32b).

Within all this cacophony, at the final dying cry of Jesus, there is one man who sees through it all. 'Surely this man was the Son of God' (v 39). Where is the emphasis in what he said? 'Surely' means 'definitely, a moment of enlightenment'. 'Was', however, implies that it's all over. 'Son of God' grants Jesus the acclaim, the title of Messiah. All this from a Roman centurion, a Gentile, far from home, simply doing his job.

What do we make of this? I've passed through many an Easter weekend, participating in worship while at the same time planning a walk, looking forward to football, anticipating the family's arrival. Maybe it's all too familiar. Maybe I need to look at these events through the eyes of those who don't yet believe, those far from home, those who yearn for purpose in their lives. For this is the turning point of history. This is when everything changes.

Find a place away from the holiday distractions. Give this passage enough time. Look at Jesus through the eyes of God, his Father. Let your eyes be opened.

BIBLE IN A YEAR: Deuteronomy 29,30; Psalm 36

Supporting Cast

As I pause, caught between crucifixion and resurrection, lead my meditation and prayer.

Were the women braver than the male disciples, or were they simply less conspicuous? Their place in the Gospel so far has usually been in the background. This is the time for them to take on a considerably more important role. Service and care are essential, if background, activities within the day-by-day ministry of Jesus and the twelve. Social mores in Palestine required that the women allowed the men to be more prominent, but they were there, and in considerable numbers (v 41b).

It's easy, also, to assume that the whole Sanhedrin was against Jesus. Social and political pressures possibly kept Joseph of Arimathea quiet during the bitter and threatened debates at the house of the high priest. Now, to avoid the ignominy of an unburied corpse on the Sabbath, he screwed up his courage and hurriedly gained permission to take down the body, wrap it in linen and place it in a secure tomb. It was his time to stand out against the crowd – and, in the background, two women looked on.

Easter Eve is a day when we pause. The painful emotions came yesterday. The joyful emotions will come tomorrow. It's a time to ponder, to imagine ourselves into the characters who, like us, were waiting. What were the men, hand-picked by Jesus, doing? Regretful, angry and confused, what did the future hold for them? What persuaded Joseph to stand up and be counted? Does the centurion play a key role in allowing him to receive the body? Who takes the lead among the women? God has no need of leading lights to move into the next act of the drama. Step forward the women whom he has chosen.

Make a mental note of those you identify as above you and below you in influence, intelligence and attractiveness. Thank God that you are in exactly the right place.

BIBLE IN A YEAR: **Deuteronomy 31,32; Romans 8**

Just as He Told You

Father, lead me gently into the wonder of your victory.

I don't understand how white light splits into a spectrum of colours. I don't understand a nuclear reaction. I don't understand the vastness of space. And I don't understand the resurrection of Jesus. I'm with those women. They arrived in a state of deep sadness, at the earliest hour, with a task to do, the final preparation of the body for burial. Heads down, they considered the practical issue of the heavy stone. They were utterly unprepared for what they met, the stone rolled away from an empty tomb and a young man waiting for them. They didn't understand.

Can we ever grasp the true enormity of the resurrection? The answer is no. It's too shattering to comprehend. It goes against the finality of death. For the women it jars with the grieving process they were going through. Their first reaction isn't a triumphant 'He is risen from the dead and he is Lord'. It's alarm, fear, bewilderment and physical shaking (vs 5,8). Given a clear commission by the angel (v 7), they fled. They didn't tell anyone. They didn't understand.

The angel's words are clear and simple. First, understand that Jesus doesn't belong here among the dead (v 6). Second, go home to Galilee, where you feel safe and secure (v 7). Third, remember what he told you (v 7).[1] In God's purposes, there is no surprise. This is how it was planned to be. This is what Jesus has tried to explain to his followers. Honestly, it's not how I would have done it. I don't understand it, but it's all in line with what Jesus said. If I am willing to follow his teaching on ethics and society and love, then I should follow this too. God's victory over death and evil that we celebrate today is overwhelming.

Read Romans 8:11. Welcome the Holy Spirit of resurrection into the day you are living today.

---

[1] Mark 14:28

BIBLE IN A YEAR: **Deuteronomy 33,34; Romans 9**